P9-ELQ-053

NORMAL

is just a setting on your dryer

Patsy Clairmont

TYNDALE

Tyndale House Publishers, Wheaton, Illinois

NORMAL IS JUST A SETTING ON YOUR DRYER

Copyright © 1993 by Patsy Clairmont

Library of Congress Cataloging-in-Publication Data

Clairmont, Patsy.
    Normal is just a setting on your dryer / Patsy Clairmont.
       p. cm.
    ISBN 1-56179-585-2
    1. Christian life—Anecdotes. 2. Christian life—1960- I. Title.
BV4517.C553 1993
242—dc20   93-3380
                                       CIP

A Focus on the Family Book Published by
Tyndale House Publishers, Wheaton, Illinois 60189

Editor: Janet Kobobel
Cover design: Al Eiland
Cover photo: Scott Gibson

Printed in the United States of America

      03 04 05/18 17 16 15

NORMAL
is just a setting on your dryer

To my mom,
Rebecca McEuen,

housekeeper, homemaker,
& humorist
extraordinaire

Contents

Acknowledgments

Writing a book is never a normal experience, nor does its completion express the efforts of just one person. It took a lot of above-normal people for this project to become reality.

My husband, Les: thank you for your love and all the creative ways you find to express it.

My firstborn son, Marty: thanks for all the hugs when I felt discouraged.

My younger son, Jason: thanks for believing the best in me and for me.

My sister, Elizabeth Vegh: thanks for laughing at my stories.

My editor, Janet Kobobel: thanks for your above-and-beyond-the-call-of-duty involvement. You are not normal; you're exceptional.

My computer specialist, Mary Lou Schneemann: thanks for responding to a last-minute, frantic call with sacrificial generosity.

My adviser, Ruth Ann Davis: thanks for your insights that you wrap in life-giving humor. You have been a healing gift to me.

Thanks also to friends who nudged, nurtured, and prayed:

Carol Porter	Nancy Berrens
David Berrens	Ginny Lukei
Jan Frank	Lauren Hess
Danya Voigt	Joanie Karpanty
Lana Bateman	Debbie Wirwille

Thank you also to Verna Paul for giving me an anything-but-normal hideaway. It was truly a little bit of heaven.

Finally, a big thank-you to Focus for including me in the family. A special thanks to Al Janssen, Gwen Weising, and Larry Weeden.

1

Normal Nonsense

L ord, if only I could be normal like other people!" That was my constant prayer during the years I hid away in my home with agoraphobia (a constricting circle of fears that leaves one housebound). Then I got out of my home, into the flow of people, and found out "ain't nobody normal." Unique, yes. Special, definitely. Normal, no way!

Normal is just a setting on your clothes dryer and has nothing to do with people. Try as we might, we remain peculiar people with distinct differences.

I was peeling tomatoes in my kitchen one day when a friend began to laugh. Surprised, I asked what was so funny.

"I've never seen anyone take the skin off tomatoes before adding them to the salad," she said. She thought that was abnormal.

But when I was growing up, my mom always removed the peel for our guests. She considered it good manners to make things special and convenient for our company. Peeling tomatoes was the norm for us.

I had a neighbor we nicknamed Mrs. Ickity-Pickity because of her seemingly abnormal need to have things clean. We used to laugh because she even washed the soap in her soap dish.

Today I don't think that's strange at all. I find it unappealing to spot a grimy gob of gooey soap stuck in the sink. It is now my normal procedure to follow Mrs. Ickity-Pickity's example and douse my Dial.

My husband, Les, not only felt it was normal to rise up early, but he also was certain other people's character was flawed if they didn't leap out of bed at the first glimmer of light. Normal for my family, on the other hand, meant that on days when schedules permitted, a late morning snooze was a treat to be enjoyed. You can imagine the conflict these two "normals" caused as they—and we—collided.

As an agoraphobic, I felt anything but normal. I didn't know of anyone else who was afraid to go to the grocery store because the aisles seemed to swallow them up. I didn't know of anyone who listened to 30 weather reports every day and then hid under the table from approaching storms. Nor had I talked with anyone who couldn't ride elevators or stay alone at night. Then when I had to give up driving because of panic attacks, I knew I was hopelessly abnormal.

Yet if you could coax agoraphobics into a room together, there would be a "normalcy" among us in that our behavior would match in many ways. Just goes to show—normal is only a setting on a dryer.

I believe abnormal is normal. Think about it. Consider your friends—great people, but don't they have some pretty curious ways? Abnormal is not an isolated occurrence but a constant reoccurrence. It's something we share in common . . . our differences.

I kept trying to attain normalcy by being what I thought others thought I should be. How exhausting! Everyone seemed to have his or her own definition of my normal, leaving me feeling like an isolated emotional abnormality.

That's what this book is about—emotions and how they affect and infect our lives and our need for a healthy balance. We'll look at a variety of emotions and how, if we deny them, we end up out of balance, and yet if we indulge them, our pendulum swings too far the other way.

This *isn't* a book on how to be normal. (I haven't figured that out yet.) Rather, it's an encouragement to be the best "us" we can. We think we know ourselves so well, yet we find our emotions often mysterious. And sometimes our emotions surprise and overwhelm us.

You may experience different feelings in response to these stories of others who struggle, fail, start over, and celebrate. You'll see that life is seldom as simple as setting your dryer to normal. And my prayer is that you might laugh, cry, think, remember, and come to understand yourself better as you move through the pages of this book.

2

Sure I Can!

Most of us over 40 find it difficult to believe we're losing our youth. Our minds are still spunky, at least in a sputtering kind of way, and tend to send inaccurate information to our bodies like "You can still leap buildings in a single bound." *Right.* I can hardly step into an elevator without having my arches fall.

At 47 (at the time of this writing), my mind is marching to "The Battle Hymn of the Republic," while my body is humming in the background, "That'll Be the Day." Even with my increasing physical disruptions, I keep holding my thumb over the birth date on my driver's license when I'm cashing a check.

My friend Claris, a heroic woman who drove school buses for 19 years and has lived to tell of it, forgot her age. It had to be amnesia that caused her to be coaxed into going roller-skating in her forties. An hour later she was in an ambulance, and she wasn't driving. A cast, crutches, and several months later, Claris was back wheeling around in her bus, which has the only size wheels she now trusts to hold her up. Speaking of holding up, . . .

Jim was certain he could reach a little higher than his arm span while tottering on the top rung of the ladder. Need I tell you any more? Our fiftyish friend came down like the Jericho walls, but instead of broken pitchers, he had broken ribs. After being taped back together, he felt every breath he took. Speaking of breathtaking, . . .

Meagan decided to take up downhill skiing . . . at 40. Her first time out she fell backward on her skis, but they didn't release. That was not good. Meagan had to be removed from the slopes on a stretcher by the ski patrol. She wore a mega foam collar for months.

You would think we would learn from our friends' examples. Well, actually I did. I don't roller-skate, climb ladders, or ski downhill. No, not me: I'm too smart to try those tricky feats. Instead, I decided to ride a five-speed bicycle. My infamous ride would have been a cinch had I ever before ridden a bike with the brakes on the handlebars, which I had not. That became quite clear to who knows how many.

My son Jason and I rode our bikes to a nearby store, where, instead of braking when the bike slowed down, I side-saddled it and jumped off like Annie Oakley. I ran into the store and bought a couple of small items. We didn't have a basket, but I was confident I could manage the bike and the bag. It had been many years since I had ridden a bicycle. (Actually, I was eight when I got my last bike.) But you know what they say: "Once you learn, you never forget."

We were almost home when my bike began to pick up speed. Evidently there was more of an incline on our street than I had realized. For a moment I felt like a kid again, with the wind whipping through my tresses and the houses passing by in a whirl of colors. Suddenly I recognized the whirling greens as my house. I instinctively pedaled backward to brake. Nothing happened. I mean, nothing happened! My acceleration was such that I could see I was headed rapidly for the side street. If my calculations were correct, I would cross it at the speed of light.

Feeling I was losing control of this ride, I kind of panicked. Then I recalled Les's reminding me, as I rode away, that the brakes were located on my handlebars, and that I should squeeze them to stop. I could only grip on one side because of the bag, and when I squeezed, nothing happened. Seeing my life skateboard past me, I grabbed for the other grip, bag and all, and pulled as hard as I could. Sure enough, something happened!

I became airborne. Over the handlebars and into the wild, blue yonder. I'm sure I looked like a 747 wide-body. That is, until my landing. I did a belly-flop glide down my sidewalk/runway, stopping just before I became a permanent design on our front steps.

Jason looked down at me in utter amazement. I'm not sure if he couldn't believe I could ride a bicycle that fast or fly that high.

If this had happened to you or you had observed it happening to someone else, what would you expect the first words out of the person's mouth to be? Perhaps "Call 911!" or "Get your dad!"

Well, that's what a normal person might say. But not me. The first words out of my swelling lips, while my face was still ingrained in the cement, were, "Is anyone looking?"

Is anyone looking! Give me a break! The sidewalk/slide had torn my pant leg off, my knee was ripped and gushing, I had skid marks on my stomach, my elbow felt like Rice Krispies, my ribs had a Vise-Grip on my lungs, and I wanted to know, "Is anyone looking?"

With Jason's help, I limped into the house, carefully lowered myself into a chair, and cried. My tears were as much out of embarrassment as from pain.

From my emotional response, I had obviously damaged something more than my body. Mine was a giveaway statement of someone suffering from fractured pride.

But then I wondered: Isn't that true for any of us who can't accept our limitations?

3

Ouch!

P ain is God's megaphone," C. S. Lewis said.

If that's true, then, folks, I've heard from heaven!

Last year I went through months that were a literal pain in the neck. I've been accused of being one, and now I know what it feels like to have one.

I hauled too many suitcases, briefcases, purses, word processors, and carryon's through too many airports and hotel lobbies. I exceeded my recommended load limit, and in doing so, I stretched my back and tendons. I then spent painful months learning the importance of listening to my body.

My physical therapist asked why it took me so long to seek medical help. To tell you the truth, I thought I was just being wimpy, and that if I kept bench pressing my luggage, eventually I would look as fit and fabulous as Stormie Omartian. Instead I complicated my recovery, as the tendon damage spread from my shoulder to my elbow, and then to my wrist.

Our bodies protest when we do things that are beyond their ability to perform. Body signals alert us in many ways. Our muscles, tendons, ligaments, and back scream when we try to lift or carry things that are too heavy.

Les is a strapping fellow who, during his younger years, was so strong (how strong was he?) he could lift buffalo. What he shouldn't have tried to carry was the two bundles of shingles for our roof. Actually, he might have achieved that hefty task if, after he slung both bags of shingles over his shoulder, he hadn't had to climb up two stories on a ladder. Even then he might have made it if, when he put his foot on the roof, the ladder had stayed still. Which it didn't. And neither did he.

The first part of Les's fall was broken by a porch landing. He then proceeded to tumble down a flight of steps and collide with the less-than-cushy earth.

Stunned, Les lay very still to assess the damage. After a few breathless moments, he rose slowly, slung the bags over his shoulder again, and climbed back up on the roof.

Les's friend Tom Wirsing had witnessed this acrobatic feat. But because Tom was on the roof when it happened, and Les took the ladder with him when he fell, Tom couldn't come to Les's aid. He spent several harrowing moments as a helpless bystander. When Les stepped back on the roof, Tom had just two words for him: "Go home!"

The next morning, Les's body was buzzing with messages. Les needed a headset to keep up with all the incoming data. His back went on strike, and his legs, sympathetic to the back's protest, filed their own grievance. Muscles he didn't know were a part of the human structure reported their existence. Bruises the size of roof tiles added color to his battered frame. The bruises served for quite a while, like Post-It notes, as a reminder never to do that again.

Along with Post-It notes, our bodies have built-in alarm clocks. Instead of waking us up, they're designed to insist on rest. These alarms go off every time our heads nod dangerously behind a steering wheel, we fall asleep in class, or we drag through a day with the enthusiasm of a yawn.

When Les and I were a young married couple (versus the relics we are today), Les worked a long way from home. One morning, as he neared work, he began to nod. We had stayed up late that week, and his need to sleep sat on his eyes like sandbags. The sound of the early-morning traffic became a lullaby, and Les took a nap. It didn't last long. He woke abruptly when he hit a parked car, which hit a parked car, which hit another parked car.

Les called me on a pay phone from the scene of the crash. "Patsy, I've been in an accident."

"Are you okay?"

"I'm not sure. My head is bleeding. Here come the police. I have to go." And he hung up.

I was seven months pregnant and beside myself with concern. I had no idea where the accident happened or if he truly was all right. My body soon announced that if I didn't settle down, our family would be having more than an accident.

Five hours later, my smiling husband walked in the door. I hugged him and cried with relief. Then I wanted to lambast him for not calling me back. It all worked out well. Les decided it was easier to hit the hay than a lineup of cars.

Mood swings can be the body's beeper, reporting possible hormonal havoc. I remember three sisters I met at a retreat who were concerned their fourth sister was in spiritual trouble because she wasn't her usual bouncy self. They kept her up late at night and prayed with her over every possible hidden sin in her life. Later they found out she was just pregnant. After a couple of months and some uninterrupted sleep, her hormones settled down, and she was back to her perky self.

I'm not saying the all-night vigil was a bad idea, but there are times when mood swings beep attention to a legitimate health issue.

There's no doubt we are fearfully and wonderfully made. All we have to do is listen to our bodies and respond with good choices. Some of you already are disciplined and wise in caring for yourselves. But, like me, many of you don't listen until you're in trouble. We could all benefit by answering the following:

How much water do you drink in a day? (No fair counting the water in coffee or cola.)

How many hours of sleep do you require a night to feel "normal"? (Les requires seven hours but prefers six. I need eight hours but enjoy nine. Les catapults from the bed each morning, while I have to be jump started just to ignite a pulse. Remember, normal is just . . .)

Do you have an exercise regimen? (Getting out of bed each morning does not qualify as weight lifting.)

When was your last eye exam? (I took my mangled glasses in last week for repair. I had sat on them . . . for the third time. The woman looked at them and said, "Lady, do you know which end these were made for?"

"Evidently not," I replied sweetly, "or I wouldn't be here again.")

Write down the date of your last dental appointment. (If B.C. follows the date, it has been too long.)

Are you listening to your body when it says, "Enough is enough" (food, work, rest)?

When was your last physical? (Talking to a friend who once took a first-aid course does not count.)

Did it include a pap smear? (This is an uplifting experience.)

Have you had a mammogram? (That's where the technician thinks she's a magician and tries to turn a cup into a saucer.)

Have you ever had a change in your weight without a change in your eating? (My mother-in-law thought she was fat. Her "fat" turned out to be a tumor the size of a watermelon. My husband was losing weight while eating like a buffalo. [Maybe that's why he could lift them.] It turned out he was diabetic.)

Are you having frequent headaches, stomachaches, backaches, rashes, sleeplessness, spotting, mood swings, urination, unquenchable thirst, and so on? It's time to find out why.

How many pills do you take in a week? in a month? Are you masking a growing health issue? (Our plop-plop, fizz-fizz mentality covers our pain but doesn't resolve it.)

Trust the way God has designed your body to let you know when you need to make a life adjustment or a visit to your family doctor. This body is just a temporary time suit. (Can't you hear it ticking?) It's the only one we get before heaven's new, improved version, which will be complete with eternal vision.

Speaking of vision, remember that in this life, your glasses belong on your nose. Take it from someone who knows.

4

Jumpin' Jehosaphat

Some friends were getting ready to move and needed a home for their dog, Fredda. We already had a dog (Fredda's mama) but felt obligated to take Fredda back since we had given her to them fraudulently. See, I thought she was a he when I gave Fredda to them, and they therefore named her Fred. After arriving home with their little guy, they noticed Fred had problems that would require surgery or a change of names. They kindly opted for a name change.

Fredda was a kind-of-cockapoo. Actually, she thought she was a kangaroo (no doubt the result of her early identity crisis) and developed a unique straight-up-and-down leap. She was a very sanguine dog and hated to be left outside. So she used her incredibly high leap to peek in our windows at what was going on. It wasn't unusual to be sitting at the table eating and, out of my peripheral view, glimpse a set of eager eyes and fluffy, flying ears. By the time I could turn to look, Fredda would have dropped out of sight. She repeated this Olympic feat frequently.

This caused many visitors concern about their sanity. We tended not to mention our "kangaroo" to guests until their eyes looked dazed. You could see them trying to process whether their minds were leaving them or we had been invaded by seeing-eye fur balls. With quick jerks, our friends would whip their heads to the side in an attempt to catch our mystifying mutt. Eventually we would confirm their UFO sightings to ease their troubled minds.

Fredda became our son Jason's dog (he was eight at the time) and would escort him to the bus stop. Jason would have to leave early because it takes longer when you're with an animal that insists on leaping up instead of forward. One morning, Jason came bursting back into the house crying, "Mom, Mom, come quick! Fredda's been hit by a car!"

I grabbed my housecoat, and as I secured it, Jason added, "I think she's going to be all right, because I saw her tail wag!"

Halfway up our driveway, a lady I had never met came running toward me and right into my arms. She was crying, "I hit your dog! I'm sorry, I'm sorry." I held her for a moment and assured her we knew it was an accident.

She sobbed, "Yesterday my cat died, and today I've hit your dog!"

"I'm sorry this has been such a painful week for you, and I know you didn't mean to hit her," I responded. I hugged her one last time and encouraged her to go on to work.

I thought how disconcerting as well as disastrous it must have been for that lady to have a flying dog, all eyes and ears, leap out of nowhere.

By the time I reached the road, Les had arrived and was gently placing Fredda in his pickup. He looked at me and shook his head to let me know she was dead. I turned to look for Jason and saw that he was back in line for his school bus. He had his eyes squished tightly shut, and his little arms were pressed firmly against his body in his attempt to not see or know the fate of his beloved, bouncing buddy.

"Jason," I said softly.

He didn't move.

"Jason, honey, your doggie is dead."

He fell into my arms, allowing the swell of tears out of his flooded eyes. Then his tense little body let down and began to shake. I took him by the hand, and we walked down the hill to our house to grieve.

Many times I, like Jason, have wanted to just close my eyes and not look at reality. Reality is often harsh, filled with unfairness, pain, and loss. But when I refuse to face truth, I find myself rigid with anxiety and unable to deal with life. Acknowledging and letting go of what I can't change is the beginning of the grieving process.

5

LOW • NORMAL • HOT

Crafty

I do crafts. No, wait, that's not quite right. I own crafts. Yes, that helps to bring into focus the blur of materials stuffed into assorted baskets, drawers, and boxes in my attic and basement.

My craft addiction has left partially done projects pleading for completion. I have snarls of thread once meant to be used in needlepoint and gnarly-looking yarn intended for an afghan. I have how-to books worn from my reading and rereading of the instructions. (I love reading; it's the doing that bogs me down.) Swatches of material, florist wire, paint brushes, grapevines, and (every crafter's best friend) a glue gun—along with a myriad of additional stuff—greet me whenever I open my closet.

Every time I'm enticed into purchasing a new project, I think, *This one I'll do for sure.* I've attempted everything from oil painting, floral arranging, quilting, and scherenschnitte (the German art of paper cutting) to quilling.

"Quilling?" you ask. For those of you unfamiliar with it, this craft requires you to wind itsy-bitsy, teeny-weeny strips of paper

19

around the tip of a needle. Once they're wound, you glue the end, using a toothpick as an applicator so your paper coil doesn't spring loose. Then, with a pair of tweezers, you set your coil onto a pattern attached to a foam board, securing it with a straight pin. You are then ready to start the paper-twirling process over again. To be a good quiller, it helps if you, the crafter, are wound loosely. I believe quillers (at least this one) have to be a few twirls short of a full coil to attempt this tedious art.

You may be wondering how many of those paper tidbits one needs to finish a piece. That depends on the size of your pattern. I chose a delicate, little snowflake. Taking into consideration that I'm a beginner (which is still true of every craft I've ever tried), I decided to select a small pattern and not overwhelm myself. (This would be like saying, "I think I'll go over Niagara in a barrel rather than a tub in hopes I won't get so wet.")

When I started my snowflake, I thought, *I'm going to make one of these for each of my friends and put them on the outside of their Christmas packages.* After five hours and a minuscule amount of noticeable progress, I reconsidered. *I will give these only to my best friends and include them in their gift boxes.*

A week later, I realized I didn't have a friend worth this kind of effort; only select family members would get these gems. And they would be all they'd get. I thought I would also include a contract for them to sign, agreeing to display their snowflakes well lit, under glass, in a heavy traffic area of their homes, all year.

Fifteen hours into my little winter-wonder project, I decided this would be the first and last paper wad I'd ever make . . . and I'd keep it for myself. It could be handed down in my family, generation after generation, in a time capsule, after my passing. I often wondered who the flake really was in this venture.

I suppose you're asking yourself, *Did she finish it?* Not yet, but I plan to (great inscription for tombstones).

I once attended a retreat where I was persuaded to join a wooden angel craft class. The angel done by the instructor (art major) as an example was adorable. Mine (craft minor) looked like an angel that might join a motorcycle gang.

Even that angel didn't get completed, because they ran out of heavenly parts. She had only one wing and was minus her halo. Actually, it was kind of sad. Today my fallen angel lies at the bottom of a box in my basement, covered with rotting quilt pieces and plastic ivy, still waiting for her ordination. May she rest in peace.

I took a painting class for credit and received an A. Finally, something I could succeed in! Of course, if that was true, why didn't I have a picture to hang?

It hit me that I didn't have a painting anyone could identify, much less display. For one of our projects, we painted apples in a bowl. When I took it home, my friend thought it was a peacock.

I approached the instructor and asked how I had earned an A in her class. "For showing up every week," she responded. She must have the gift of mercy.

Les and I started hooking a two-foot-by-three-foot rug 25 years ago. We're almost to the halfway point. We figure, in a joint effort, that we have hooked less than an inch a year and should complete it in the year 2012. You may want to get on our gift list.

I seem to be more into ownership than completion . . . and then I feel guilty. I've noticed I'm not alone in that. Some kindred spirits could stuff a landfill with their forsaken artistry. I wonder if that's why we have so many garage sales and so much garbage in this country. We sell off and throw away our unfinished business, and then we go buy more.

Words like *responsibility, follow through,* and *moderation* get lost in the shuffle as I push back one box of crafts to move in my newest project. Every time I haul out or hide away another abandoned endeavor, it reinforces a negative quality within me.

Besides, what happened to the notion "Waste not, want not" ?

That's a great line. I wonder how it would look in cross-stitch? Oops, there I go again.

6

Snappy Answers

ometimes I feel as though my emotions are a tangled wad. I guess that's why one night, while I was in bed praying for a creative way to visualize emotions, I thought of knotting rubber bands together. I jumped up and found a bag of 100 red, blue, green, and yellow rubber bands. Then I climbed back in bed and began to tie them in a long, snarled chain (probably the closest I've ever come to knitting or crocheting).

My husband came into the room and saw me busy at my stretchy task. He shook his head and muttered, "I knew one day it would come to this."

I often ask my audiences if they brought their emotions with them to the retreat. Usually they giggle, and a number of women raise their hands, signifying they did. Then I ask how many of the gals brought their hormones, and the rest of the hands go up.

When I next pull my emotions out of a bag in the form of my rubber chain, the women titter and nod their recognition. I demonstrate, by tugging at the bands until they appear they will snap, how people sometimes get on my nerves. As I pile the

long, variegated snarl into a five-inch-tall heap on my hand, I
show them what happens when I don't stay current with my
emotions—they become so entangled that I can't tell what I'm
feeling. And when I can't identify what I'm feeling, I can't
resolve it, which means the knotted mess is growing inside me.

I remember coming home one evening after being with a
group of friends and telling Les how angry I was with one of
them.

"Really, what did she do?" he inquired.

Well, I told him in no uncertain terms what she did.

When I finished, he said, "I don't think you're angry."

"You don't?" I asked.

"No," he reinforced.

"I feel angry," I assured him.

"I think you're jealous," he stated boldly.

"Jealous?" I screeched.

"Jealous?" I hissed.

Then I slunk into another room to file my nails in private.
Alone, I finally asked the Lord if what Les suggested could possibly be true. Immediately I realized he had caught the cat by her
claws.

I've been able to work through my jealous feelings in regard
to this friend thanks to Les's confrontation. Otherwise, I'd still be
rationalizing my anger and not facing the real issue.

When issues aren't faced, they build inside us, which means
somebody's going to experience emotional whiplash when we get
crossed. The way buildups become blowups is that one day a family
member, co-worker, friend, or total stranger makes one teeny-tiny
comment, and we let that person have it with our entire rubber-band
arsenal. He or she doesn't know what happened.

When the person asks, "What's wrong with you?" we shout, "Everything!" shaking all our tangled emotions in his or her face.

Have you ever noticed how quiet a room gets when you over-react? All eyes are on you. Even though no one says it, you know they're wondering what your problem is. But then, so are you, because more often than not, the time and place where you explode are side issues.

I once had a disagreement with a co-worker, and when I came home, I started nit-picking on my teenager Jason. I hit him with a lengthy list of criticisms. Baffled, he asked, "What's wrong with you?"

Those words caught my attention, and I realized I was the one with a problem. Jason was the victim of my misdirected frustration.

Sound familiar? Does to me.

I find that when I have a gob of feelings overlapping, I begin to highlight one or two emotions. I then work those feelings over-time and ignore the rest. That's why I thought I was angry with my friend instead of jealous. Besides, jealousy is so—so—well, petty, whereas anger is more respectable (righteous indignation) and gives me a feeling of being in control.

I find it fairly easy to say to someone, "My friend Jane makes me angry." (I'm in control.) But it's hard to confess, "I am jealous of Jane." (Now I feel vulnerable, and that's scary.)

For years, I majored in fear. I seldom felt another emotion during my agoraphobic days. I was afraid of everything, or so it seemed. Later, I began to get in touch with anger, joy, sadness, and other equally important feelings. As I identified them, my wad of rubber bands became smaller. That gave me more inner space for the things of God.

What is your most-frequently-expressed emotion? Do you find yourself erupting in anger? enveloped in fear? engulfed in guilt?

If we don't deal with our raggedy strands, we react like turtles — our answers have a bite to them, and then we pull our heads back into hard shells of denial until our next snappy performances.

7

Step Right Up

I can identify with Zacchaeus in that I have a difficult time finding a place high enough to let me see a parade. Visibility is limited when you're five feet tall. I've spent a lifetime on my tiptoes, calling up to others, "What's going on?"

I know I'm supposed to take comfort in the saying "Dynamite comes in small packages." But I don't want to blow up; I want to grow up.

Sitting tall is also a challenge because invariably, a seven-foot-two fellow will plant himself in front of me at church. I then have the joy of staring for the next hour at the seams in his shirt and his nappy neck. It's like trying to watch a ball game through a billboard.

Hugging is often a strain as we shorties have to reach past our stretching points to squeeze a neck. It's such a rumpling experience and requires readjusting everything from hat to hose.

As a speaker, I frequently find myself peeking over lecterns in my attempts to spot the audience. It's difficult to retain the interest of people when their view consists of your forehead and eyebrows. I have stood on many creative booster stools so I could see and be seen.

At one retreat, the kitchen workers brought me a box of canned juice to stand on. It worked fine until my high heel poked between two cans and I jerked sharply backward. I grabbed the lectern, catching myself just before doing a topsy-turvy somersault. My disheveled appearance from my stage aerobics made me look juiced.

I have perched on many piano benches to speak. Because they're pieces of furniture, I always remove my shoes before stepping up. Smooth nylons on shiny-finished wood equal slick chick in action. It's like trying to speak on ice skates—possible but risky.

To elevate me enough to be seen at one church meeting, the staff quickly piled up two stacks of hymnals, five deep. As I turned to look at my audience from one side of the auditorium to the other, the books would swivel. At one point, the right-foot stack headed east while the left-foot stack headed west. Those shifting stilts kept me divided in my concentration, as I was concerned I would leave with a split personality.

I've stood on milk crates, suitcases, tables, and kiddie stools. Once I was precariously placed on a wooden box whose weight limit I obviously exceeded. It creaked threateningly throughout my presentation. As I closed in prayer, a soloist began to sing, and I cautiously stepped down. Relieved that I hadn't burst the boards, I walked down the platform steps to take a seat. At the last step, my heel caught in the microphone cords, and I crash-landed in the front row as the singer was belting out "Amazing Grace." I obviously was not Grace, although in a discussion later, we thought it was amazing I could survive my teeter-totter platform and then splat when I arrived on solid ground.

It's difficult to be taken seriously when you're 60 inches short. People have a habit of referring to shorties as "cute." "Cute" is what you call a toddler, a house without a future, or the runt of a litter.

I tried to increase the presentation of my stature by wearing tall clothes. But more than once while walking up the front steps in sanctuaries, my heel slid into the hem of my long skirt, toppling me across the altar, where I looked like some sort of short sacrifice.

I shortened my skirts and added shoulder pads to my jackets in an effort to give an illusion of tallness without tripping myself.

Then one time I was in Washington, and when I was introduced, I grabbed my suit jacket and slid into it as I headed for the stage. I had been speaking for about 15 minutes when I turned my head to one side and noticed that my left shoulder was four inches higher than my right. Evidently the pad, rather than conforming to the shape of my shoulder, perched on it. Up to that point, I was the only one in the auditorium who hadn't noticed. I was speaking on being dysfunctional and suggested this perched pad was proof of my expertise in the subject.

When I finished speaking, the mistress of ceremonies approached the steps with the back of her dress tucked into her pantyhose. That took a lot of pressure off me.

Another time, I was sharing the stage with a statuesque and elegant friend who, as I was speaking, noticed my mega shoulder pad had slid off my shoulder and into my blouse. She reached in through my neckline and fished down my back in her attempt to retrieve it. I was stunned but continued to speak as if I didn't notice she was shoulder deep into my clothing. Well, I lost the audience as everyone became hysterical watching her catch my illusive inches and pat them securely back into place.

I wish my height were my only struggle with smallness. Unfortunately, I'm also shortsighted in my faith. I'm one of those "If I can see it, then I can believe it" people.

Zacchaeus was a small man who shimmied up a sycamore tree to give himself a boost. To that extent, I can identify. But his next move made the difference for him in a way lengthened robes or mountainous shoulder pads under his togas never could. He inched out on a limb to glimpse the Savior. He risked the shaky-limb experience of faith and responded to the Lord's invitation not only to come down, but also to grow up.

That day he stepped down from his own efforts to see and be seen and stepped up to the call of the Lord. Zacchaeus still lacked inches, but he gained insight and walked away a giant of a man.

Faith is a believe-it-first proposition, with no promise I'll get to "see it" regardless of how many boxes I climb. That's scary . . . like going out on a limb, huh, Zac?

8

Short(s) Circuited

Knowing my friend Nancy is like embracing a waterfall. She splashes over with energy, excitement, and enthusiasm for life and people. She's filled with joy, and also mischievousness. Her mind and wit are quick and memorable. David, her husband, is a courageous man who has survived and been blessed by Nancy's outrageous humor. We all remember when . . .

David is mellow and usually cooperates and enjoys his wife's wishes and whims. But one day the two of them had a tiff, and neither Nancy nor David would budge from the feeling of being in the right. Several days had passed since the difference between them arose, and static hung in the air, droning out communication.

David would normally give in under such circumstances, but not this time. Nancy was amazed he wasn't talking, but she was equally determined not to speak first.

Then it happened. David came home and started to pack his suitcase. Nancy was confident he wasn't leaving her; he was often sent on business trips. But she couldn't believe he would go without resolving their conflict first. David, however, jaw set, silently prepared to leave. Nancy fumed.

Most of us, when we fume, have to verbally spew so we don't become combustible and explode. Not Nancy. She uses her hostility to create . . . well, let's just say *memories*.

That night, they went to bed without a word. David was feeling a slight advantage in their "cold war," because he knew what his travel plan was, and she didn't. He also knew this would bug her, because she's a detail person and likes to be fully informed. David fell asleep that night with a smirk on his face. I don't think he would have rested as well as he did, however, had he seen the grin spreading across his stalemate's lips.

David rose the next morning and went in to take his shower. While he was washing up, Nancy was quietly yukking it up. First she counted his undershorts in the suitcase to see how many days he would be gone. Finding that out, she then could determine where he was going. He always went to one of two places, each requiring him to stay a different length of time.

Once she figured out his destination, she quickly lifted the neatly folded underwear out of his luggage and replaced it with a note. Stifling giggles, she stashed his confiscated shorts in a drawer, zipped his case closed, dashed back between the bedsheets, and used a pillow to muffle her pleasure.

David emerged showered and shaved, picked up his suitcase, and left for his trip. This was the first time they had parted company without hugs, kisses, and promises to call. They were both finding a bit of comfort, though, in thinking they had a secret the other didn't know.

The outbound flight put David in a confined place with time

to think. He began to feel bad about their stormy week and his stony departure. He dearly loved Nancy and promised himself and the Lord that he would call and apologize as soon as he arrived at his hotel.

Nancy meantime busied herself around the house, stopping occasionally to imagine David's reaction when he unpacked. Chuckling, she waited for the phone to ring, both dreading and delighting in the prospect.

She didn't have long to wait. "Mom, it's Dad; he wants to talk to you," her son yelled.

Nancy wasn't sure if she should run to the phone or run for cover. But she made her way to the table and picked up the receiver. What she heard was not what she had anticipated. On the other end, David confessed his regrets at their spat and expressed even greater sorrow at leaving without making things right.

Nancy's heart sank as she was warmed by his tenderness and sincerity. She decided she had better 'fess up, too.

"David, have you unpacked yet?" she inquired.

"No, not yet."

"Maybe you should," she suggested.

"Why, what did you do?"

"Just go open your suitcase; I'll wait on the line."

David came back chuckling. "Very funny, Nancy. Where did you put my shorts?"

"Oh, they're here in the drawer," she admitted.

"No, really, are they in a side pocket?"

"Honest, I took them out before you left. Isn't that funny, David?" she said with failing confidence.

The line was silent, and then, much to her delight, David

broke into gales of healing laughter.

The note? Oh, yeah, it read:

"David, your attitude stinks, and now so does your only pair of underwear!"

9

Middle Man

Because of a delay in taking off, my homebound flight was late, leaving me at risk of missing my second plane. When we landed at the connecting airport, I did an O. J. Simpson through the terminal, arriving at my gate just as they were closing the doors. Relieved I'd made it, I headed down the aisle in search of my seat. I stopped at my assigned row and, to my dismay, found I had the middle seat.

There are some things I don't do. Middle seats head my "no way, I ain't gonna!" list. Middle seats make me feel like an Oscar Mayer wiener advertisement. My mood swing went from "I'm so grateful I caught my plane" to "I don't care what this ticket says, I'm not sitting in that center seat!"

I glanced around and realized, however, that this was the last available seat on the flight, and I would sit there or on the wing. Previously I always had an aisle seat; this just wasn't normal. All things considered, though, I prayed for an attitude adjustment. I remembered that God will operate on our attitudes but that He requires us to cooperate.

To do my part, I tried to think of a way to make this irritating situation fun. I took a quick survey of my seating again and thought, *What could I do with a person on each side of me?*

Then it came to me that I could pretend I was Oprah Winfrey and my seat partners were my guests. I would interview them. Now, this had possibilities!

Right off, there was a problem. Evidently the lady by the window didn't recognize my Oprah impersonation, because she wasn't a very cooperative interviewee. She was reading a book, and she let me know with sighs and downcast eyes that she didn't want to be disturbed. I thought Oprah wouldn't allow that to stop her, so I continued.

"Are you married?" I inquired.

"Yes," she mumbled.

"Do you have children?" I persisted.

"Yes," she grumbled.

"How many?" I pushed.

She stared at me with a strange look on her face, and I thought maybe she didn't know. Then she leaned in to me, lowered her voice, and said, "Nine."

"*Nine!*" I bellowed, surprising even myself. "Nine," I repeated, this time to myself. I don't think I had ever met anyone with nine children before . . . and she was pregnant. I was impressed!

Now, I also have this problem in that whenever I'm given noteworthy news, I feel led to pass it on. As I sat there trying to mentally contain those nine children, it seemed as if a balloon was being blown up inside me. I would explode soon if I didn't tell someone about these kids.

I leaned back toward the woman and said, "Would you mind if I tell this man on my left that you have nine children?"

Startled, somewhat confused, and slightly irritated, she whispered, "If you feel you need to tell that man!"

"Trust me," I responded, "I need to do this."

I then leaned to my left and said, "Excuse me, I thought you might like to know that this woman has nine kids."

"*Nine!*" he exclaimed, leaning forward to view this productive female, much to her consternation.

That was the kind of enthusiastic response I was looking for. I decided right then that he was a kindred spirit, and I turned my interview efforts toward him. Besides, I now realized that Multiple Mom was too pooped to participate in my game show (she had nine good reasons to be).

I had already observed something about this young man when I was being seated. He called me "Ma'am." At the time I thought, *Either he thinks I'm ancient, he's from the South, where they still teach manners, or he's in the service.* I decided the latter was the most likely, so I asked, "You in the service?"

"Yes, Ma'am, I am."

"What branch?"

"Marines."

"Hey, Marine, where are you coming from?"

"The Desert Storm, Ma'am."

"No kidding? The Desert Storm!" Then I thought, *This interview stuff is great!*

"How long were you there?" I continued.

"A year and a half. I'm on my way home. My family will be at the airport. I'm so scared." As he said this last, he took in a short, nervous breath.

"Scared? Of what?" I asked.

"Oh, all this hero stuff. I'm not a hero, I'm just me, and I don't want my family to be disappointed."

"Take it from me, Marine, your parents just want you to come home safe."

Nodding his head in hopes I was right, he looked at me and asked, "What do you do?"

I had been waiting for someone to ask this very question. I had just completed my first book, and I wanted to announce that I was an author. Here was my big chance. Sitting as tall as a five-foot person can, I said clearly and possibly a little too loudly, "I'm an author."

"An author! An author!" the Marine proclaimed. "An author," he repeated, obviously impressed.

I loved this kid!

Changing the topic back to him (as Oprah would do), I commented that he must have thought about returning to his family and home many times while he was in the Middle East.

"Oh, no, Ma'am," he replied. "We were taught never to think of what might never be, but to be fully available right where we were."

What great instruction, I thought, *whether you're in the armed forces or the army of the Lord.*

Then Michael (that was his name) told me that when he lived at home, he and his mother were friends. When he joined the service and was stationed in Hawaii, they had written to each other and had become good friends. But when he went to Desert Storm, they became best friends.

"She will never know how she affected my life while I was away," he continued. "I've never thought of myself as a religious person, but while I was in the Storm, I learned to pray. The example I followed was the one my mom set for me when I was growing up."

"What was the most difficult time for you?" I inquired in Oprah fashion.

"There was a four-month space when we had not seen a woman or a child. The day we drove into Kuwait was very emotional for us. The women stood in the doorways, waving, but even more moving was when the children ran to greet us," he said, his voice still filled with the feeling.

I wondered if the children affected the soldiers so deeply because children give us such a sense of a hope and a future.

"Since I've been stateside waiting to go home," he continued, "I've been thinking about my nephews, and I can hardly wait to hear them call me Uncle Michael. The title *uncle* means even more to me than being called *sergeant*."

About that time, the flight attendant was passing by, and I tugged at her skirt. She looked down, and I said, "Know what? He"—I pointed toward Michael—"is returning from Desert Storm, and she has nine kids." I gestured in the direction of Super Mom.

The attendant evidently knew people with nine children, because that didn't hold her attention. But Michael sure did. She asked him several questions and then requested that he write his name on a piece of paper. Taking his signature, she headed toward the front of the plane. She reminded me of a woman with a balloon inside her that was ready to pop.

Moments later, the pilot came on the intercom and, with enthusiasm and sincerity, said, "It has been brought to my attention that we have a VIP aboard. He is a returning GI from Desert Storm."

Michael groaned and began to inch down in his seat.

I sat up taller.

"Sergeant Michael is in seat 12F," the pilot continued.

All heads swung in our direction. Michael had slunk so deeply into the upholstery that he was about two inches tall. In contrast, I was six-foot-two. (Visibility is always good for ratings.)

Then the pilot said, "As a representative of this airline and a citizen of the United States of America, I salute you, Michael, and thank you for a job well done."

At that point, the entire plane burst into applause.

Wow! I love this Oprah stuff.

The pilot came back on and said, "We are making our final approach into the Detroit Metro Airport."

Michael's breath caught.

I looked up and saw his eyes had filled with tears. He peeked through a tear to see if I had noticed, and of course there I was, goggling at him.

He said softly, "I just don't want to cry."

"It's okay," I told him. "I checked a Marine manual on this one, and it's all right to cry. Some of the most admirable men I've ever known have shed tears at appropriate times, and Michael, this is a right time."

"Then you don't think I need to blame this on my contacts?" he responded, grinning.

"I don't think so," I said with a giggle.

As our plane taxied in, I told him the best gift my son brought me when he returned from 18 months in Guam was that after he made his way through the waiting crowd, he scooped me up in his arms and held me for a very long time.

It was time to deplane, and when Michael stood, men all around us slapped him on the back and pumped his arm, thanking him for his contribution.

We made our way to the front, where the pilots came out to meet the sergeant and shake his hand. The flight attendants encircled him and told him he was great. I noticed that he didn't seem to mind this last gesture. In fact, he seemed to be getting taller.

Because of security precautions, no one was allowed to meet us at the gate, which meant we had to walk down a long corridor before we reached Michael's family and my husband.

Michael's homecoming included a lineup of relatives armed with video equipment, flags, cameras, and banners. When we were close enough for eyes to focus in and distinguish which one was Michael, his family began to chant, "Michael, Michael, Michael."

Michael stopped dead in his tracks. I got behind him and pushed. "C'mon, soldier," I said, "this isn't the enemy. This is your family."

He started walking again, but his shoes seemed to be full of cement, and he was moaning quietly with every step.

Even from a distance, I could identify his mom. She was the one leaping the highest in the air. A guard leaned against the wall, watching to make sure no one stepped over the security line. But every time Michael's mom jumped into the air, she came down with her toe just over the line to let that guard know who was really in charge.

As we got closer, she stopped jumping, and her hands went over her mouth to muffle the building sobs. Tears poured down her arms and dropped off her elbows . . . just over the line.

I realized that this was not my party (or Oprah's) and I needed to step back. When I did, in his nervousness, so did Michael.

I gave him a final nudge toward his family, and they engulfed him, everyone in tears.

I made my way through the other waiting people, wiping my eyes. When I saw my husband, he spotted me dripping emotions. "I'm part of this," I sniffed, nodding toward the reunion.

"You think you're a part of everything," he proclaimed.

That was true, but this time I really was . . . sort of. I wanted to stand and watch as I saw Michael find his mom in the crowd and pull her into his arms and hold her.

"That's tacky, Patsy," Les reminded me. "It's rude to stare."

Mr. Manners guided me over to the escalator and prompted me on. I turned backward so I could watch for as long as possible. As the moving steps drew me away from the celebration, I saw Michael still holding his mother, and he had held her for a very long time.

When we got to the baggage claim area, I prayed for the first time ever that my luggage would be delayed. Before long, the whole Desert Storm entourage came down to claim Michael's duffle bags.

Yes! I thought. *My big chance to be part of the finale.*

Michael was still surrounded by family when I saw a youngster toddle over and pull on his pant leg. I realized this must be one of the nephews he was so eager to see again. When I noticed how young the boy was and remembered that Michael had been gone for a year and a half, I held my breath to watch how the boy would react to his uncle. (I thought about my sons when they were that young and how, if I left them with a sitter for more than an hour, they acted as though they didn't know me when I returned.)

Michael's face lit up as he reached down and picked up the young boy. His nephew wrapped his chubby legs around the sergeant's waist, and his arms encircled Michael's neck. Then the boy's mom came over, and I heard her ask, "Honey, who's got you?"

He looked up, his young eyes reflecting his hero, and said, "Uncle Michael."

I could breathe again.

A few minutes later, as Les escorted me to the car, the thought hit me that I almost missed being a part of this tender event because I hadn't wanted to sit in the middle.

I wonder how many divine appointments I've missed because I found my circumstances not to be what I expected (just not normal), and my defiance robbed me of His greater plan?

10

Yuk It Up!

We all have moments we'd rather not remember—the kind that when we do recall them, we get embarrassed all over again. Like finding you're dragging a long sweep of toilet tissue. Spike heels are great for that. You shish kebab the tissue on your way out of the restroom, and you can literally parade it for miles before anyone will tell you.

Having dragged my pantyhose behind me through my hometown has left me with empathy for other dragees. I remember a gentleman and his wife who approached me at a convention and related their adventure.

The man said, "If you think it's embarrassing for a woman to drag her pantyhose, how do you think a man feels when it happens to him? I went to work and walked through the office when one of the women sang out, 'What's that, Bill?' I turned to look, and dangling out of my suit-pants leg were my wife's pantyhose. I casually ambled over to a wall, shook them out, and walked away. I left the hose huddled in the corner to figure out their own transportation home."

Evidently his wife didn't pick up her pantyhose, but the static in his slacks did. Half the hose clung to his pant leg, while the remaining leg danced behind him. The man, his wife, and I laughed long and loud as he relived his tail.

There's something so healing about laughter. When I can laugh at an event that has the potential to turn my pale face flashing red, somehow the situation doesn't record itself in my memory with as much pain.

My friend Ann is a good example. She flipped her melon and lived to laugh about it. While she was shopping for groceries one time, she spotted a large, elongated watermelon. She wanted the melon, but it looked heavy, and she wasn't sure she could lift it. No stock boys were around, so she decided to give it the old heave-ho. Either the melon didn't weigh as much as she had thought, or she was stronger than she realized. Anyway, she grabbed hold of the watermelon and slung it up and toward herself. With torpedo speed, the slippery melon slid out of her hands and up her shoulder to become airborne.

Once again, Sir Newton's theory of gravitation proved true. The melon headed for earth with great rapidity. When a melon is dropped from more than five feet onto a tile floor, "splat" doesn't begin to describe what occurs. Not only did it explode, but everything in a 15-foot radius was affected as well.

As Ann turned to look at her Herculean effort gone awry, she spotted . . . a victim. Or should I say the victim was "spotted"? A nicely dressed businesswoman looked stunned as ragged chunks of watermelon dripped down her pantyhose.

Ann didn't mean to laugh, but the whole scene struck her as so absurd that she couldn't help herself. The lady was not laughing, which seemed to tickle Ann all the more. The woman marched off in a huff, leaving a trail of seeds behind her.

Ann was now leaning against the rutabagas, trying to catch her breath, when the manager walked up and said, "This is not funny."

Well, that was the wrong thing to say. Poor Ann howled. Her sides were splitting, her face was red, and she was hysterical. She said she was trying to gain her composure so she could find the lady and apologize to her. But finally she had to just leave the store.

Laughter can make moments more memorable. Whether laughing alone or with others, it helps us feel good about our memories.

I remember walking through the mall once when I noticed a quarter on the floor. Had it been a penny, I might have passed it by. But a quarter? No way. I stooped down and swooped my hand across the floor to scoop up the coin, but it didn't budge. I tried again. I could hear laughter coming from a nearby ice cream shop, but I didn't look because I was focused on the shiny coin. I tried to pick it up again, but it held fast. I tried prying it with my nails. I even took out my emery board and used it like a crowbar, trying to dislodge this gleaming coin.

As I stared at George Washington's immobile silhouette, I thought I saw him smirk. Then I realized George was not alone. The laughter nearby had grown to unbridled guffawing. I looked up and realized five teenagers were watching me and laughing at my financial struggle. It was the kind of laugh that told me they knew something I didn't.

I could have flown off in a fury or resented their intrusion. Then again, I could find out what was so hilarious and join the fun.

I asked, "Okay, what's the deal?"

One girl confessed they had glued the quarter to the floor and had been watching people try to pick it up. The kids dubbed me the "most dedicated to the task." I giggled with them as I thought about my 25-cent antics.

Laughter is an incredible gift. It helps us to not take ourselves too seriously and makes it possible for us to survive life's awkward moments.

11

LOW • NORMAL • HOT

There's a Reason

When my high school teacher's eyes suddenly met mine, my heart began to palpitate. I slowly slid down in my seat, trying to disappear inside my open textbook.

"Patsy," she sang out, "let's hear your report."

This was not music to my ears. During my school years, I had developed creative avoidance skills in an ongoing endeavor to escape up-front presentations. Not making eye contact was a crucial part of my strategy. In a careless moment, however, I had glanced toward the chalkboard, only to find myself in eye-lock with this dear but determined teacher.

Realizing I would have to respond, I slowly rose and, on knees of silicone, made my way to the front of the room. My topic was "Quinine."

Fear had collected in my throat, which I forgot to clear before announcing the title of my speech. The "Qui" came out like the deep rumblings of Mount Saint Helens, and the "nine" screeched at a pitch that attracted dogs from three counties.

The class howled. My face flashed lipstick-red. I speed-sputtered through the report, never looking up.

By the time I finished, the jelly in my knees had congealed into blocks of cement. With 50-pound knees, I stiffly hobbled back to my desk. I plopped into my seat, dropping my eyes in humiliation. For the remainder of the semester, I studied the designs in the tile floor, not daring to glance up lest I be called on again.

When people don't make eye contact, there's a reason.

I had been cleaning my bedroom and headed for the kitchen to find the glass cleaner. As I passed through the living room, I glanced in the direction of my two-and-a-half-year-old (at the time), Marty. He had been watching cartoons and playing with his cars. Something about his looks made me stop in my tracks. I realized it wasn't what I saw but what I didn't see—his eyes. Marty stared down at his toys. I called out, "Marty."

He lifted his head but avoided my eyes. I walked toward him, and he sheepishly peeked up at me. Then I saw it. Lying on the floor behind Marty was an open bottle of baby aspirin. Little, pink pills were strewn among his playthings. I pulled Marty to me and looked into his mouth. Crushed aspirin particles were stuck in his tiny, white teeth. My heart began to pound wildly.

This was a new bottle of medicine, and only a few tablets had been used before now. I scooped up the remaining pills and quickly counted them. It appeared Marty had ingested 69 aspirins.

I drew him into my arms and ran to my neighbor's apartment. We didn't have a telephone, and Les had taken the car to work. I ran into Sharon's home and frantically called my physician. The woman who answered the phone instructed me not to bring Marty in but instead to induce vomiting by running my finger down his throat. She informed me that the doctors were too busy to talk to me. I thought, since she worked for the doctors, that she must know what was best, and I followed her directions.

I hung up feeling sick to my stomach but with a sense of urgency rushing through my mind. I dialed my mom's number and yelled, "Marty has an overdose of aspirin in him! Help me!" I slung the phone down without waiting for an answer and ran with Marty in my arms the two doors back to our apartment.

When my mom arrived, I was in the bathroom working with my little guy. It was necessary to do what I was doing to him, but very unpleasant for both of us. Mom and I took turns helping him bring up the potential poison until, in one effort, Mom's fingernail jabbed his tonsil, and Marty started to spit up blood.

Mom and I were unsure if we should continue, so we picked him up and ran back to the phone. This time I was able to speak directly with the doctor. He was appalled to hear we had been told not to come in. Now too much time had passed, and the aspirin remaining in Marty had gone into his bloodstream. The doctor said to let him play but to watch his eyes and not let him go to sleep. He said that if Marty's breathing became difficult, we should rush him to the hospital's emergency room.

I hung up the phone, and as I was telling Mom what the doctor had said, Marty's eyes closed and his breathing became erratic. I firmly shook him awake, and we headed for the emergency room.

That had to be one of the longest nights of my life. The hospital wouldn't allow me to be with Marty, so I camped out all night in the waiting room. By daybreak he was out of danger. Mom and I had been able to get enough of the medicine from his system that he had no long-term damage. But it would take him a while (us, too) to recover from the trauma of this event.

When we returned home, I investigated how Marty had managed to get to the aspirin. We didn't have childproof bottle caps at that time, so as a precaution, I had placed the bottle in the highest cupboard of our home. Marty, however, had ingeniously pulled a high stool over to the cupboards and climbed up on it, taking along his play golf club. From what we could determine, he had then stepped up on a shelf and, while holding on with one hand, swung his club, knocking the bottle off the upper shelf. The drop must have loosened the top, and the rest, as they say, is history.

What alerted me to our emergency was not the stool or golf club but Marty's eyes—especially when he wouldn't look at me.

When people won't look at you, there's a reason.

I can tell when my friend is angry at her husband, because she won't look at him. She avoids visual acknowledgment of his existence until he somehow works his way back into her favor.

Others aren't sure of what to do with how they feel, and they find themselves dodging eye contact to avoid giving away their hidden emotions or getting into conflict. Lack of visual involvement is a screeching smoke detector, alerting us to smoldering relational issues. How many times have you heard or said, "If you're not upset, why won't you look at me?"

Some folks are so full of shame that they don't feel worthy of personal eye contact. Then there are those who have been traumatized and feel frightened and abnormal. They only allow themselves quick peeks at those around them.

Guilt can be another visual barrier that keeps people from our view. Whether false or genuine, guilt affects our connection with others.

The way I see it, when people won't look at us or we won't look at them, there's a reason!

12

Heigh-ho Silver

I love playing word games, though Les would rather go to the dentist and have all his teeth extracted than join me. So once a year, whether he feels like it or not, we play a game of Scrabble. That is, until . . .

It was twilight, and we had been playing a short time (hours if you asked Les) when our eight-year-old, Jason, questioned, "What's that noise?"

I was in eye-lock with my letter tiles and didn't even look up. Les, who had been staring at the ceiling counting cobwebs to entertain himself, took an immediate interest in Jason's noise just in case it offered him a way out. Sure enough, it did.

Jason went to the window, and then, with eyes the size of saddles, he hollered, "The horses are out! The horses are out!"

That broke any concentration I had, as we all rushed to the window to see for ourselves. Our hearts began to pound, and we stood frozen for a moment. We watched as a dozen horses stampeded across our yard and toward the road.

The potential for disaster sent everyone scrambling. Les yelled for our oldest son, Marty, and his friend Steve to try to head them off. The boys hightailed it out the back door, and Les sped out the front.

I, being of great value during a crisis, ran back and forth in the house, shouting, "Oh, my! Oh, my!"

Then I went out on the porch to peek, but I couldn't see what had happened because the horses had galloped out of our tree-lined yard and onto the well-traveled road. But I could hear. Screeching tires first, and then a sickening thud, followed by breaking glass. A shudder went through my body, and my mind kicked into high gear.

I flew back into the house and phoned our friend Tom across the lake. "Come quick! The horses, ran, road, thud, glass . . . ambulance, vet, tow truck . . . Come quick!" I sputtered like a stenographer.

Panting, I made my way out to the line of trees, but I was too scared to look. Jason leaned out to see what had happened, and I snatched him back. "No, Jason, this is too gruesome for a child. Go back to the house," I instructed firmly. Then, considering the wisdom of those words, I went with him.

By the time I reached the front door, Marty and Steve were coming up the hill after corralling the remaining herd. Then Les walked in, shaking his head and mopping his brow. He proceeded to explain the runaway results.

It seems a neighbor was on his way home from work when he came over the top of the hill by our house. As he crested the hill in his Volkswagen, all of a sudden he was part of a stampede. He hit his brakes, and as he skidded, his little car scooped up one horse, slung it over the roof, and gently deposited it back on the road, heading in the opposite direction. As the horse skimmed the top of the rounded vehicle, it tapped its hoof through the passenger's window, leaving splintered glass piled neatly in the empty seat.

The car came to a stop long enough for the uninjured but dazed driver to regroup and then drive home (with quite a "guess what happened to me on the way" tale to tell). The rattled runaway, wide-eyed and wiser, was ushered back to the barnyard to rejoin the rest of the herd.

Les and the boys had just caught their breath when up drove Tom and his troops. His wife, Joyce, their kids, and some friends had all piled in the car to see the horse-rendous accident and do what they could to help.

But now the car, driver, horses, and even the glass were all gone. The road was humming with traffic, the horses were grazing innocently in the pasture, and Les was lounging next to the Scrabble board . . . grinning. It appeared to be a normal evening at the Clairmonts'.

Our friends looked at me as if I had imagined the whole thing. I began to wonder myself. Les finally confessed, but only after I released him from any future spelling games.

When emotions stampede like wild horses in the night, one may end up with hoof prints in one's mouth.

I had made assumptions based on what I had heard but hadn't actually seen, and then I had passed on that information. I had the sinking feeling this wasn't the first time I had done that.

13

Clean Sweep

Feeling zonked, I decided to zone out when I boarded the plane bound for home. I found my row and secretly checked out my seat companion. She was a normal, fifty-ish-looking woman. (I immediately liked her for being older than me.) I peeked at her so I wouldn't be obligated conversationally. I didn't want anything to disrupt my siesta in the sky.

Doesn't it just drive you bonkers when you have a hidden agenda and someone toddles into your space and trips up your plan?

This time my "toddler" was a flight attendant who came scooting down the aisle offering treats. My stomach won out over sleep, and I ended up chatting with my neighbor, Susan. Am I glad I did! This was no normal woman.

Susan told me an incredibly sad story with a surprise ending. She said her beloved husband of 30 years decided he loved someone else and wanted a divorce. The feelings of crushing betrayal deepened when Susan found out his affair had been going on for years. He was also a clever businessman and had prepared himself for this decision so that he would come out the financial winner.

Susan was first numb and then paralyzed by her grief. Her husband used her shock to his advantage, swooping down fast and furious to get all he could. Much to Susan's dismay, she was notified by the court that she would have to turn over to her husband and his girlfriend her cherished home of 23 years, where they had raised their five children.

Reeling from grief upon grief, Susan moved into a tiny, furnished apartment. There she tried to figure out what had gone wrong. In the divorce settlement, she was awarded a small, failing business, and that was to be her source of income. To add not only to her dilemma but also to her pain, her ex-husband and his female friend opened a new, competing business just down the street.

Now, folks, I don't know about you, but that's where I would throw up my hands and spit.

Not Susan. She reached inside and pulled up her faith. She decided she couldn't allow others' choices to extinguish her joy or decree her future. She was determined not to be a victim but to be victorious and begin with a grateful heart. No, she wasn't grateful for her tremendous loss, but that God is a healer of fractured hearts.

One day while doing dishes, Susan turned on the small TV near her sink. As she changed channels, she came to a musical presentation and was caught up in the contagious melody. But now she had no dance partner.

Then she spotted her companion leaning against the cupboard. He was the tall, silent type. She waltzed over and embraced the kitchen broom, then twirled about the room, laughing and singing. Around and around she spun, dizzy with delight. Suddenly she realized she was not alone.

Susan saw she had been joined by three of her married daughters, who were standing in the doorway, giggling at their mother's antics. (They checked on her regularly those days for fear her losses would be more than she could bear, driving her to an act of despair.)

As she stood holding her silent partner, Susan looked at her girls and said, "In the years to come, may this be the way you remember me . . . dancing."

Susan didn't want to leave a legacy of brokenness or despair. Instead, she chose to give a living heritage of courage, conviction, and, yes, celebration. Her circumstances were anything but normal, but then, so was her response.

By the way, she was able to turn the little business around, buy a lovely home, and enjoy a full and active life. She chose not to stay in her sorrow or linger in her loss, but in the midst of devastation, to dance.

14

LOW · NORMAL · HOT

You-Turn

I am always going. Going places, going to town, going up, going down, and even going bonkers. But one going I don't do well is going back. I'm a forward person, and I'm married to a fast-forward kind of guy. If Les and I are pulling out of our driveway and realize we've forgotten something after we've passed our mailbox (affixed to our front porch), we don't go back; we go without.

Since I'm an "Onward Christian Soldier," you can imagine how difficult it is for me when I have no choice but to go back.

Janet, a friend, and I had just completed four glorious days of study and fun. We stayed in a beautiful, wooded setting that we thought was paradise. The grounds were complete with English gardens, wild turkeys, deer, and swans.

The most attentive creatures were the swans—especially the male fowl, who truly was foul. He changed our thoughts forever about swans' being gentle beauties. Good-looking he was; good-natured, guess again.

We nicknamed him "Dick the Bruiser." Dick's walk was an

overstated strut. He would flex his chest feathers and then swagger. To further intimidate us, this bully would stretch out his S-shaped neck until it became an exclamation point. The feat made you wonder if there were a giraffe in his family closet. He seemed to be of the mind that the grounds were his and we were intruders. After he backed us into the kitchen and didn't allow us to leave until he finally became bored with us, we decided it *was* his place. We did our best to stay out of his way the rest of the time we were there.

When it came time for Janet and me to leave, we were reluctant because it had been a perfect writing place for us. With the Bruiser's permission, however, we eventually packed the van and said our good-byes. We hugged Zona (the best cook in Michigan), waved to Dick and his willowy wife from the safety of the van, and hit the dusty trail.

We had a three-hour ride in front of us, and we decided to use the time brainstorming. Janet and I had been chatting for an hour when I noticed my gas gauge was registering a little skimpy. I chose to fill up then to prevent any delays later.

I swung into a country service station and ordered ten dollars worth of gas. Then I reached for my purse. It wasn't there. I panicked. Janet prayed. Then Janet paid. No purse, no moolah.

I pulled away from the pumps, parked the van on the side of the road, and began a frantic search. I rummaged through the boxes, bags, and baggage in an attempt to force my purse into existence. While I ripped apart the van, Janet was nervously tossing animal cookies into her mouth.

I finally had to admit I had forgotten my handbag back with the Bruiser. Ol' Beak Face was probably picking through it while I was ransacking my vehicle. (I wonder how swan feathers would work for pillows?) To make matters more frustrating, buckets of bone-chilling rain were coming down.

Looking for an easier answer than going back, I decided to call Les. The only available phone was an unprotected one that I couldn't reach from the van. So I jumped out into the downpour and grabbed the receiver, only to realize I had forgotten my home number. I jerked open the van door, my hair hanging down my face like wet feathers, and asked my California guest if she knew my number.

Janet was still munching morsels. (I don't think she was hungry but thought it best to chew on the cookies rather than chew me out.) She dipped into her purse and pulled out my number. She tried reading it but instead showered me in hippo crumbs. I took the sticky scrap with the scrawled numbers and hurried back to the phone. I reached Les as the rain washed away the writing, leaving the paper as blank as I was feeling.

After a quick but soggy talk, Les and I agreed I would have to return to claim my belongings. I sloshed my way back to Janet, who appeared to have stored the cookies much like a chipmunk storing acorns in his chubby cheeks. I announced my backtracking plan to her. She swallowed hard and smiled weakly.

Once I made the U-turn and aimed the vehicle in the "wrong" direction, we tried to cheer up. We remembered we had passed a bakery advertising homemade pies. We had valiantly declined the chance to have a piece on our first drive by. Now we agreed we should not only stop, but we should also each have our own pie as a source of comfort. In preparation for this highlight, we talked about what kinds we hoped they had, and we tried to imagine the light, flaky crust.

Our mouths were watering when we spotted the bakery ahead.

I sped up and turned into the driveway, only to spot something else. The bakery had closed. I began to wonder how swan pie might taste.

I know an hour's distance is not that far, but when I have my mind set on forward, I find it exasperating to switch directions. My mistake added two unnecessary hours to our travel. With each mile back, we felt the emotional impact of going the "wrong way."

Janet was kind and didn't say I was a nitwit. But I found it difficult to forgive myself for this stupid stunt.

"If only I hadn't left my belongings," I whined repeatedly. Yet my purse was too valuable not to retrieve. It was full of my identification, as well as my finances. I had to drive the long road back before we could continue our journey.

I find this is also true when we're working on issues from the past. We have to be willing, at times, to look back so we can go forward. If we don't, we leave valuable pieces of our identification behind.

It's not unusual to feel angry about going back to retrieve our emotional "bags," because most of us have our indicators set on forward. Returning seems like such a waste of effort. But it's the same as when I recovered my purse; once I had what was mine in hand, my anger began to subside, and I was more fully equipped to move ahead.

The temporary inconvenience of returning put me in a much better place than if I had gone home and arrived there both angry and without my personal belongings.

Unresolved childhood conflicts can leave us in cycles of anger, guilt, shame, or fear. Those feelings use up more of our time than if we made the ride back and took care of our personal stuff. They also add stress to our relationships, leaving us stuck in negative emotional cycles without an exit.

Angie felt like a mouse in a maze. She was caught in her unmanageable emotions, and she couldn't find a way out. Her husband, Rich, was exhausted from trying to understand her and was threatening to leave.

When Angie first called me and confessed her bizarre behavior, I suggested she talk to a counselor about some childhood pain. She instantly became irate, declaring, "My childhood was like being brought up in Ozzie and Harriet Nelson's home. It was perfect."

Angie's strong response indicated that the past was a painful and scary place for her. Her proclamation showed an extreme need to avoid not only going back, but also checking her rearview mirror. Her reluctance to consider yesterday as an answer for today was as normal as my hesitancy to backtrack for my bag.

Later, out of desperation for her own emotional well-being and for the sake of her marriage, Angie made the journey "home." She claimed "her belongings," which turned out to be far more valuable than she had imagined. She also felt a sense of inner relief, making it possible for her to move ahead.

The strange thought patterns and behavior that had plagued her lessened and then stopped. When Angie was able to change channels (from "The Nelsons"), life came into clearer focus for her. She began to tune in to reality and see how her life actually had been. Living in truth, although initially painful, helped her emotions to heal. Today Angie enjoys healthier thoughts and improved relationships.

Back is, at times, the most forward step we can take.

15

LOW · NORMAL · HOT

Accidental Perspective

I bounded out the door, energized because I had completed a writing project and motivated by a purchase I was going to make. I had been working on a story for two days, and it had finally come together. While I was writing, in the back of my mind, I kept thinking about a used piece of furniture I had seen in town that would be just right for my office. I needed a book and display case, and this piece offered both, plus more. The price was right, too.

I was excited as I headed into our little town full of delightful shops offering wonderful "deals." I was almost to my destination when, in my rearview mirror, I noticed a car come up behind me at a fast clip. I remember thinking, *That guy is going to hit me if I don't scoot out of his way.* I added a little pressure to the gas pedal and turned my wheel to hurry into a parking space. That's when it happened. A loud thud was followed by crunching, scrunching, grinding sounds as my minivan rearranged the front fender of a parked car.

I am of the belief that if you're going to hit a vehicle, you should select one with someone inside. When you smack an empty, parked car, you pretty much rule out the chance the other person may have been at fault. All eyes are focused on you. Also, if you must have an obvious accident, it's better not to do it on Main Street in your hometown.

I jumped out of the van and ran over to look at the smooshed car. The victim's vehicle had two silver beauty marks streaking down the side, and the chrome fender curled out instead of in, giving it a flared appearance.

Then I ran inside an office and asked if the car belonged to anyone there. It didn't, so I headed for the next building, when I heard someone call my name.

A lady I had just met at Bible study two weeks prior waved and ran across the road in my direction. She gave me a hug and told me everyone in the ladies' dress shop heard me hit the car and came to the window to see what had happened and who had done it. When I had stepped out of my van, she had squealed and announced, "I know that woman!" In a small town, anonymity is difficult.

Then she added as she checked out the crumpled car, "You could tell this story at conferences."

Trust me—at this point, I was not eager to tell my husband, much less the world, what I had done.

I dashed into the shop where the bookcase was and called to the clerk, "I have to go turn myself in at the police station, but would you please measure the bookcase for me? I'll be right back to purchase it."

As I headed for the front door, I heard a sweet voice say, "I just sold it."

"No!" I exclaimed. "You don't understand! I hit a car in my attempt to get here and buy this piece" (as if that would make a difference). Then I whined, "The buyer wasn't driving a dark blue Buick, was she?"

The saleswoman assured me she wasn't. I could tell she felt bad about my situation, but I felt worse. On the way to the police station, I thought, *Maybe I'll have them throw me in the slammer and sleep off this trip to town.*

When I arrived, I confessed to a woman behind a barred glass window that I had committed a crime. She called for an officer to come and write a report. While I was waiting, I noticed the zipper on my pants was down and my red shirttail was sticking out like a road flag. I quickly turned away from the men sitting in the waiting area to "fix" myself and tried not to think about how long my red tail had been waving. A fleeting recollection of me looking like Wee Willie Winkie as I ran from one store to the next, trying to find the car's owner, darted through my head.

The officer appeared and began to ask questions. Near the end of the inquest, he asked, "How much damage did you do to your vehicle?"

"I don't know," I answered.

"You don't know?" he echoed.

"I don't know," I validated.

"Why don't you know?" he pushed.

"Because I didn't look."

"Why didn't you look?" he asked in disbelief.

"I'm in denial," I confessed.

"You have to look," he told me. Then he sent me out to get my registration.

I returned, paper in hand.

"Well," he said, "how much damage?"

"Sir, I didn't look," I said with polite resignation.

He shook his head and gave me back my registration. As I was leaving, I heard him say, "You'll have to look."

When I got home, I asked Les to go out and look.

It turned out I had swiped her car with my running board. The board wasn't off, yet it wasn't on. It was neither here nor there but suspended in air. Threads at each end dangled the board precariously.

Afterward, I realized that when we spend too much time looking in our rearview mirrors, we may hit something right in front of us. Looking back is an important part of conscientious driving, but it's not the only safety precaution.

Likewise, it's important for us to benefit from our past, but we don't want to get so stuck staring at yesterday that we collide with today in a destructive way.

Unlike the situation with my van, I can't send Les to check my past and assess how much damage was done. That's my responsibility. As the officer said, "You'll have to look." But once I take care of what I can do to repair the past, I then need to drive on, benefiting from occasional rearview references and perspective.

16

High Flyer

When my brother-in-law, Bryan, was sent to Saudi Arabia during Desert Storm, my sister, Elizabeth, and their three children came for a visit. Elizabeth and the youngsters—Steven, eight; Nicholas, two; and Lindsey, four months—stayed for five weeks.

It didn't take me long to decide that combat gear would be helpful not only in Saudi, but also at our place. It had been a long time since Les and I had experienced young ones for days on end, and we had forgotten how much energy they're capable of expending. The visit also highlighted Les's and my need to consider a retirement village . . . soon!

Elizabeth, being a conscientious mom, strapped on her Reeboks every morning in her attempt to keep up with the fast-paced, creative escapades of her little munchkins.

In my effort to be supportive of this never-ending challenge, I invested in some baby furniture. First, I bought a small crib, then a highchair, and lastly a walker.

I had noticed Nicholas, the two-year-old, thought his four-month-old sister, Lindsey, made a cushy trampoline. So I thought I would spare her little body squash marks by tucking her in the walker.

When I arrived with the walker, I was eager to try it out. Fortunately it didn't require assembly, and all I had to do was open it up and slide her in. Seemed simple enough. Little did I realize I was under surveillance for the purpose of sabotage.

I innocently turned my back on the open walker while I stooped down to pick up Lindsey. In that unguarded moment, the saboteur, Nicholas, catapulted his two-year-old frame into the walker. He then pulled it up like a pair of pants and tore off running at a high speed that set the walker legs flapping in the breeze.

Much to my amazement and horror, Nicholas headed for the stairway. He evidently thought the word *landing* meant "runway" and the term *walker* was a code name for Lear Jet, because he ran right off the landing into midair.

At that point, Nicholas learned a scientific concept . . . gravity. Nick and his floppy-fitting flying machine dropped into the stairwell, crashing on the cement floor below.

My heart stopped for the split second of silence that followed. Then my feet began to gallop as screams came trumpeting up the steps. As I neared the landing, I envisioned Nicholas in a pile of little broken bones. But what I met was an enraged consumer stomping up the stairs, registering the loudest complaint I had ever heard. Evidently Nicholas wanted money back on this faulty piece of equipment.

Nicholas didn't have a mark on him and didn't even seem to be in pain . . . but he was livid this contraption didn't fly. I tried to console him, but he was intent on revenge. He kicked the plastic tires a couple of times and called it names in toddler jargon. I believe he referred to it as a "swachendinger." Finally, we were able to divert his attention while Les stowed the abused apparatus.

I find it interesting how young we learn to blame something or someone else for our behavior, and then how long we hold onto the habit. The other day I saw a grown man behaving much like my little nephew. The man's car had a flat tire, and when he stepped out of the vehicle, he proceeded to kick the tire and bang the hood with his fist. I'm glad my windows were up and I couldn't hear the names he was calling his car from his adult arsenal.

That scene was both funny and sad. Here was a grown-up conversing with an inanimate object as he tried to beat it senseless. Smart, huh? And yet he's certainly not alone . . .

A friend came over one day, steaming because the bank had dared to bounce her check. "Did you have money in the account?" I asked.

"That's not the point," she insisted. "I've done business there a long time, and they should have overlooked it."

Instead of seeing her poor bookkeeping and spontaneous shopping sprees as the problem, she pointed an accusing finger at the bank's "unfriendly tactics."

My check-bouncing friend, the flat-tire man, and my flying nephew found it easier to shift blame than to see how their actions played a part in the outcome. Blame is a common defense. I know, I've used it. In fact . . .

Recently I was running a little late for an appointment. Just before I ran out the door, I stopped to put away my mail. I noticed an unopened letter and took additional moments to open, read, and write a quick response to it.

On the way to the meeting place, I ran into heavy traffic and then had to wait at a train crossing for 100 cars to chug by. When I arrived at my destination, I was stressed out and frustrated. I heard myself accusing the stand-still traffic and the stretched-out train for my delay.

As I thought about it later, however, I realized that if I had left when I should have, I would have missed the train and had enough leeway to inch through the traffic and still arrive on time . . . minus my jangled nerves. I find that I'm often guilty of creating the chaotic atmosphere that sets me up for emotional frenzy.

In the blame game, everybody loses, and nobody changes.

17

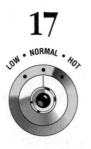

My Way

Joanie had a magnetic beauty. People often stared at her out of admiration. She also had a spunky personality and was known for being a little headstrong. Her dynamic beauty and bouncy determination made her quite popular.

Jeff was a successful businessman and real-estate investor. He was brought up in a dysfunctional home, but he had chosen a different life-style from his family's. He was well respected and loved by his friends and co-workers. When Joanie and Jeff married, everyone felt they were a perfect pair.

Joanie and Jeff had it all, with one exception. They were unable to have children. This grieved them both, but especially Joanie, who felt she had let Jeff down. Jeff remained devoted to her, but she became preoccupied with her infertility. She wept often. Her housekeeper, Karen, would hear her cry and try to console her. Karen's gentle care touched Joanie's heart, and they became friends. Joanie found herself confiding in the other woman.

Joanie and Karen's lives were very different. Karen was much younger, she lived a meager life-style, and she had only been in the U. S. a short time when she began to work for her wealthy employer.

As the months passed, Joanie's desire for a child only increased. One day, as she watched Karen arrange flowers in a vase, an idea swept through her mind. At first she was startled at her own thought, but as she entertained the idea, it began to comfort her.

Joanie wanted Karen to have Jeff's baby. That way Jeff would have a child, and Joanie would not have to live with the nagging feeling of failure.

Artificial insemination had not yet been perfected, and Joanie felt she had waited long enough. Besides, she knew Karen and Jeff loved her, not each other. So how could it hurt?

Both Karen and Jeff agreed to Joanie's plan. In fact, neither seemed to hesitate or object. And so it was that Karen became pregnant with Jeff's firstborn.

Joanie initially was pleased with her decision. But then she noticed a change in Karen's attitude toward her. At first Joanie thought she was imagining the change. Or maybe it was just the mood swings of a pregnant woman.

But time told a different tale. Not only did Karen's tummy puff, but so also did her pride. Karen felt superior to her childless friend.

Joanie was first crushed and then livid. In a fit of fury, she fired Karen.

Jeff, Joanie, and Karen's lives had turned into a tragedy. What started out as the perfect pair seemed to end as brokenness and despair.

Actually, there's more to this story, much more. If you'd like to see the end of the saga, look in an age-old book, the Bible

(Genesis). Joanie (a.k.a. Sarah), Jeff (a.k.a. Abraham), and Karen (a.k.a. Hagar) are presented in all their sadness and eventual celebration.

It's a story that tinges the reader's heart with sorrow over their choices but gladdens the heart over God's grace.

When you think about it, this trio doesn't sound old. In fact, Sarah, Hagar, and Abe's choices remind us of the tabloid headlines we see as we move through the grocery store checkout. This proves once again that Scripture offers counsel generation after generation.

"There's no new thing under the sun."

18

Flight 326

I had just finished a demanding three days of teaching in Indiana and was headed for my home in Michigan. As I stood in the airport looking out at the runway, I became aware of how exhausted I was. But I comforted myself with the thought that I would soon be home.

While standing at the window, watching for my plane, I noticed a tiny Tinker Toy-type plane putt up and park at a gate. I told myself, *See, Patsy, things could be worse. Instead of being just tired, you could be booked on that pretend airplane.*

As that thought crossed my mind, I heard an airline hostess announce my plane's arrival. I picked up my belongings and headed for my gate. Even my purse seemed heavy as I dragged along. When I arrived where I thought I belonged, I noticed I was all alone. I backtracked to the check-in desk to ask about my gate. The lady behind the desk told me that someone would be escorting me and some others outside.

Confused, I asked, "Why would I need to go outside?"

"To board your flight," she said dryly.

"I don't understand," I replied, feeling mentally deficient. I thought, *Surely I can't be so wiped out that I'm unable to process what this gal is saying to me.*

She spoke slowly, hoping, I'm sure, that a light might go on signifying someone possibly was home. "Your plane has arrived," she reannounced, directing my attention to the window. "We'll have someone take you out to board."

My eyes followed her outstretched arm, but I couldn't see my plane. I thought my mind had left me, and now my sight was impaired. I decided to be blunt. "I don't see my plane," I said, bewildered.

"Aren't you on flight 326?" she inquired.

I looked at my ticket and verified by bobbing my weary head up and down. Evidently she felt sorry for me, because she took me by the arm, walked me to the window, and pointed to the plane.

Suddenly I came to life. It was as if someone had stuck my finger in an outlet. She was aiming her sinister finger at the play plane I had seen earlier.

"No, I don't fly in anything but a jet," I shot at her.

"You are today," she smilingly bubbled back.

"No, no, there's been a mistake. I only fly in normal airplanes." I stammered the words, starting to panic.

She seemed to take my "normal" statement personally. She told me I could call my travel agent on the pay phone, and then she turned and walked back to her desk and the waiting line.

I was nauseated. How could this have happened? Then I heard the announcement that the guide was ready to take us outside to board.

Not knowing what else to do, I followed several businessmen

out to the waiting plane. The Bible verse "All we like sheep have gone astray" came to my trembling mind as I followed on the gentlemen's heels. When we arrived at the portable steps, I knew by seeing it up close that this was what is referred to as an "aircraft." That means, "something a couple of space cadets glued together in their garage while watching Big Time Wrestling."

I had to bend down to enter the aircraft. (Excuse me, but I'm only five feet tall.) Then I made my way (a distance of 12 inches) to my seat. Because of restricted space, I had to embrace my purse and briefcase in my lap. I could feel the vibration of the engine shaking my armload of belongings. Then I realized the engine wasn't running yet, and what I felt was my own pounding heart ricocheting off my clutched parcels.

I peeked around and noticed the men aboard didn't seem comfortable, either. They looked like sumo wrestlers bent forward and stuffed into seats not designed to hold them. Their knees seemed to be growing out of their chins.

The cockpit was open to us, and it appeared that if the pilot got into any problems, we, the flyees, could lean forward and take over.

I peeked out my lens-sized window as an airline employee approached the propeller and gave it a mighty whirl. I was not encouraged to know this apparatus had to be hand wound. The engine kicked into an ear-deafening rhythm.

Instead of just vibrating, I now felt as though I were being shook silly on one of those weight-reduction belts. The plane wobbled out to the runway and began to taxi. (I wished at that point that I was *in* a taxi.) I had the distinct feeling, as we sputtered ahead, that the businessmen and I would each have to sling out a leg and paddle to get this baby airborne.

That wasn't necessary. Suddenly a hose broke loose outside the plane and spewed liquid across our windows. The tiny craft reduced speed and hightailed it back to the terminal.

The next thing we knew, the pilot and copilot had evacuated the plane. Their desertion removed any question about whether they planned on going down with the ship.

Somehow, when the pilots left us, we passengers were in no mood to stay. One of the pilots ran around to the side of the plane, wiped his finger through the liquid, and smelled it. Then he disappeared.

A businessman looked at me and said, "It's a good thing none of us is smoking."

That pretty much did it for me. I was getting off if I had to stuff myself through the porthole window next to me. That wasn't necessary, though, because an airline worker opened the door at that moment and asked us to quickly evacuate the plane. I gave new meaning to the word *quickly.*

As we gathered inside the terminal, we were told there would be a short delay while they fixed the plane. I could just picture them pushing this craft back into the garage so the space cadets could safety pin the hose back in place.

In about 15 minutes, they lined us up and marched us back to the Tinker Terminator. Only now there were fewer of us, because several men refused to get back on.

That was the most purging ride of my life, as I asked the Lord to forgive me for every offensive thing I had said or done. All this confession was in preparation for meeting Him, which I knew I was going to do at any moment. The flight felt as if we were sky surfing. And then we made a roller-coaster drop from the sky, thumping onto the runway.

Les told me he was looking out the window, watching for my plane, when Tinker bounced in. He said that out of boredom, he was watching the handful of people squeeze out of the hatch when I emerged. "Boy," he said, "was I surprised to see you in a plane like that!"

"You!" I squealed with weak knees. As we walked to the baggage area, I Velcroed myself to Les's arm. I was grateful to be back on earth with my husband and my squeaky-clean heart.

Interesting how disruptive events can give us a more grateful perspective and a renewed commitment to our families and faith. Could that be what they were designed for?

19

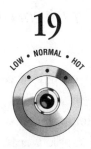

Hold Your Tongue

When Janet and I arrived at the house in the woods to work on a manuscript, the bear rug in the living room caught our immediate attention. It was large, furry, and cuddly looking. But when we viewed our new friend from the front, our assessment changed. The black bear didn't look so friendly with its huge head and ferocious, open, growling mouth. We dropped "cuddly" from our list of descriptives.

Janet and I tried to guess what might have caused this bear to look so testy. Maybe someone had swiped its Smoky the Bear poster, or perhaps it had sat on a hive and the bees had made their point. Finally we decided this was a she-bear, and someone had criticized her cubs and ticked her off. Her gleaming teeth were bared as though she were seething with anger and eager to rip off someone's limbs. But we both agreed the most despicable feature of this animal was her long, glistening tongue. Yuck!

After hours of concentration on our project, my head felt clogged with words, and my mind was skipping beats. Janet and I were losing our enthusiasm and focus. That wasn't good, because we had a lot of writing to accomplish before proclaiming our work complete.

As the gaps in my thinking process widened, I began to hit wrong keys and misspell simple words. It was obvious I needed a break.

I pulled away from my computer and walked across the room, being careful to inch around the intimidating animal skin sprawled on the floor. I shuddered as I passed. Pulling a couple of tissues from the Kleenex box, I turned to say something to Janet while walking back to the table. My eyes were on her, and for a split second I forgot our fiendish floor friend. In that unguarded moment, my foot slipped into the bear's open jaws, sending me catapulting over its head. The tongue flew out of its fierce mouth and slurped down my leg as I screamed in disgust. Trying to catch my balance, I staggered against the fireplace and cringed as the tongue slid to my feet.

Janet howled!

I broke my grisly gaze to look in Janet's direction, and we both came unglued. We laughed and laughed, the kind of laughter in which it's hard to catch your breath, and your insides jostle around like an unbalanced washing machine on spin cycle. Tears cascaded down our now-blotchy faces. Gasping, I jumped around in an attempt to jump-start my breathing. As we both caught our breath, we noticed the bear staring at its own taunting tongue lying three feet from its head, and we burst into laughter again.

After our 15-minute seizure of guffawing had passed, we felt great! The laughter had amazingly flushed our heads, refreshed our attitudes, and relieved our emotional humdrums. Janet and I went back to work with renewed interest and creative results.

Laughter lightens the load.

20

???'s

God asked a lot of questions in Scripture. That intrigues me. He who has all the answers, asked. Did you ever wonder why?

For instance, the Lord called out to Adam and Eve after they had sinned and hidden from His presence, "Where are you?"

Whenever I've read that portion of Scripture, I've wanted to tattle and call out, "They're hiding behind the blaming bush!"

The bush must really have been a dandy hiding place if our all-knowing, all-seeing God didn't have a clue to their where-abouts. I'm sure it was a big garden, but c'mon, we know God knew. So why did He ask?

The Lord questioned Eve in regard to her disobedience, "What is this you have done?"

Do you actually think God was stumped? I wonder why He didn't just dangle in front of her guilt-ridden face a Polaroid snapshot of her and the enemy dining on fruit flambé. Or run an instant replay of Adam's eating out of his wife's hand.

I notice God didn't stop asking questions in the garden but

continued throughout Scripture. Curious response from a sovereign God who can not only tell us what we've done, but also expose the content of our thoughts and hearts. Consider Hagar . . .

Hagar was in trouble. Death was knocking at her door, as well as at her young son's, when the angel of God called to her, "What is the matter with you, Hagar?"

Isn't it rather obvious, especially for an overseer like an angel? Hagar and Ishmael were a couple of crispy critters after crawling in the scorching sun. The only moisture was the boy's tears, and they evaporated before they could drip off his face.

Maybe the angel was wearing shades or was momentarily blinded by the sizzling sun. But wait, something even stranger happened next. Before Hagar could give the angel an update on her ordeal, the angel mapped out her future, answering his own question.

I'm getting more confused. If the inquiring angel knew the answer, why did he ask?

Let's see, we have Eve in arrears while the enemy leers, and Ishmael in tears while Hagar sears. Boy, do I have questions.

The story of Elijah doesn't help. Elijah had a fiery faith until Jezebel doused his flames. Jez Fed-Exed Elijah her plan to snuff him out. Elijah's faith flickered, allowing fear to flame up, and he fled.

We find Elijah headed for high ground in an attempt to control his own destiny. He was pursued not by the enemy but by the questions of God.

"What are you doing here, Elijah?" the Lord probed. Not once but twice, He asked Elijah what He already knew.

Even in the midst of death, God asked questions. We find Ezekiel in a valley of death, meandering among the corpses. The voice of the Lord solicited what sounds like advice from Ezekiel when He asked, "Can these bones live?"

Excuse me, but He who formed our skeletons from the dust of the earth and breathed into mankind the breath of life wasn't sure if the bones could live? Perhaps He misplaced His recipe. Can you hear Him pondering, *Was it one part dust to every three breaths, or three parts dust to every one breath?*

I think not. I'm the one left pondering.

God sent us His Son, Jesus. The family connection is obvious, because Jesus, our Answer, came asking questions. Like Father, like Son.

The Lord asked impetuous Peter, "Who do you say that I am?"

Still later He penetrated Peter's heart with the words, "Do you love Me?" Evidently the Lord thought Peter was hard of hearing, because He repeated Himself, "Do you love Me?" Twice I can see, but the Lord pushed Peter a third time. "Do you love Me?"

This loving interrogation left Peter stumped. He responded as we might have, "Lord, You know all things; You know that I love You."

What I hear Peter saying is, "Why are You asking when You know me better than I do?"

If we truly believe the Lord knows us, we must realize these questions have a purpose. And it certainly isn't that the Lord is forgetful and needs us to remind Him. Nor is He stuck and in need of our feeble insight. I think He questions us so we might think—think through our choices, our responsibilities, and our beliefs.

Maybe, if we try to answer some of these questions in regard to our own lives, we will better understand their wisdom:

"Where are you?"

"What is the matter with you?"
"What are you doing here?"
"Who do you say that I am?"
"Do you love Me?"
"Do you love Me?"
"Do you love Me?"

Well, what do you think?

21

Risky Business

My husband is a risk taker. Usually that has enhanced his life. Occasionally, though, his on-the-edge attitude gets him into a jam. And I'm not talking strawberry preserves.

One day Les was working on a project that required him to do some welding. In his desire to expedite things, he took a risk and didn't wear his safety glasses. He thought it might not matter since it wasn't an involved welding job. *Nyet.* It mattered.

The tingling in Les's eyes began about ten o'clock that evening, but he decided to brave it out. The sandpaper feeling began about eleven. He thought he could endure it. The feeling of hot coals sizzling his eyeballs hit about midnight. He finally requested to be taken to the hospital or shot, whichever was fastest. I debated and then settled on the hospital.

We lived at a Boy Scout reservation in the country at the time. Our two young sons were asleep, and they both had school the following day. I decided to call in a friend to take Les to the clinic. I chose our dear friend and pastor, Marv. (Don't you know how thrilled he was to receive this honor.)

Les and Marv had been friends for years. They share a common interest in getting the other's goat. They are both playful, fun-loving fellows who genuinely care for each other, although the casual observer might think there are moments when their jokes outweigh their caring.

Marv came immediately, extending concern and support. After arriving at the hospital and going through an eye check, Les learned there was no permanent damage. The doctor filled his eyes with cooling salve that immediately eliminated the pain. Then he taped Les's eyes closed, covering them in bandages that wound around his head. Les looked like an escapee from King Tut's tomb. The doctor instructed him to leave the dressings on for eight hours.

Picture the opportunity this gave Marv—Les blindfolded and needing Marv to lead him around. Marv guided Les to the parking lot and then let him go, suggesting Les find the car. It was now 1 A.M. There were only three cars in the lot. Les couldn't find any of them. (Remember Pin the Tail on the Donkey? Les's childhood training in this important game must have been inadequate. Car trunks and donkey rumps alike eluded him.) Marv finally ushered Les to the vehicle and brought him home.

At 2 A.M., I heard laughter rolling in through my bedroom window. I was dozing, waiting to hear the outcome. I had expected the best, but I was not prepared for laughter.

I pulled back the shade and saw Marv holding onto Les's arm. Marv was telling Les how to avoid obstacles in his path.

I head Marv say, "There's a step, Les; lift your foot."

Les lifted his foot in blind obedience. But there really wasn't a step, which left Les high-stepping it around the yard like a drum major.

Marv and Les were both guffawing, although Marv seemed to be laughing harder.

After I received the good news on Les's eyes, Marv headed home. We listened as he chuckled his way out to his car. Les and I laughed our way to bed.

The memory of that night could have been an eyesore for us all. But thanks to Marv, as we think back on it, we smile rather than wince. A little levity applied at the right moment can be a balm that lasts longer than the hurt, soothing a heavy heart. And yes, Les found a way to pay Marv back.

22

Blue Light Special

Moving? Not again!" That was my first reaction when Les suggested we go house hunting. After 23 moves in 30 years, I could hardly grasp the thought that it was time to pack another U-Haul. For years we had worked in camps where we lived on the grounds in camp housing. But Les felt we should buy our own home.

Purchasing a place sounded exciting, exhausting, and scary. This was to be our "grow old together" home. That meant I had better be sure I loved it, because I probably would spend a good long spell there.

I decided to make a list of everything I'd like in a home. I started my lineup with a maid, a cook, and a masseuse, but then the words "Get real" came to mind, so I chucked that list and began again.

Location was important to both of us. We had been living in the country the past five years, which was glorious in many ways but had a few disadvantages. For instance, like the pioneers, going to town was a big deal for us. That may have been due to the wagon-train-sized ruts in our road. The ride jostled you so hard, your cheeks bounced up and down and hung like jowls by the time you disembarked.

Also, we had a large hill just before our home. During the winter it could be treacherous, often causing guests to leave before they ever arrived, as their vehicles glided backward down the icy incline. During the summer, the hill made us a target for every storm that blew through our county. The winds rattled windows and snapped power lines, plunging us into darkness in the middle of the woods. Dark darkens in the woods—trust me.

I decided to wait till glory for my next mansion on a hilltop. For now, I wanted to stand by my man on level ground.

I knew I wanted a first-floor master bedroom and bath, as well as a first-floor laundry room. (I wanted Les to have easy access to the laundry in case he ever felt led to clean up his act or mine.)

Next, I thought a pantry and a dishwasher (which I had never owned before) would be great. I knew a fireplace would be fun. We'd had them before, but it had been eight years since the last one. I missed all the ashes, soot, log chips, scorching sparks, and the smoke when the flue wouldn't stay open. There's something romantic about a fireplace.

I also wanted a shower separate from the tub. Don't ask me why; I just did. A yard with trees seemed important, and I love porches. We hadn't had a garage in years, so I added that to my wish list as well. Then I jotted down a basement, because they're valuable for storage and shelter from storms. I wanted all this with a blue-light-special price tag.

As I clutched my "all I want in a house" paper, we began our search. We looked at all kinds of homes, always feeling hesitant for one reason or another.

Then, as we were driving down a street in town weeks later, I noticed a vacant home. Les took down a phone number off a building permit and called. We found out the house was for sale and had not been listed. The builder offered to show us the place in an hour. The home was not new but one a tree had squashed, and the builder had made it like new.

When we stepped into the home, my husband's face lit up. For him, it was love at first sight. I was "in like" with the house but certainly hadn't decided I wanted to live there. After the tour, Les was ready to sign on the dotted line, while I was still trying to remember what color the carpeting was. In the evening, we placed a deposit on the home, and I felt numb.

The next day, we took another walk through Les's house to see where we would be spending the next century of our lives. As Les paced off the property line, I sat on the floor of the living room, staring. Then I remembered my list, which had been buried in my purse when this whirlwind house purchase occurred. I shook out the wrinkled and crummy paper and started to check my requirements.

First-floor bedroom, check. Well, at least I did have that. In fact, it was the largest bedroom we had ever had. It had a door that opened into the first-floor bath, which isn't exactly what I had in mind, but it worked, so I checked that one also. The separate shower was incorporated into the home . . . on the second floor.

Pantry. Hmmm, I was thinking walk-in. This one had a bifold door with a single line of shelves. It was a pantry. Check.

Hurray, a dishwasher! It pleased me to check it off.

First-floor laundry, check. Of course, it was only large enough for the washer and dryer. I was thinking it would be nice to have space for things like the dirty clothes and a basket. I couldn't deny, though, that there was a laundry area.

The home had a basement, check . . . a Michigan basement. That means that once your furnace and water heater are in, it's full.

The garage sits in the backyard and will hold Les's tools and our boxes of storage. No room for a vehicle, but still a garage. Check.

Porch, check. Seats two people.

Trees, double-check. Yard is three inches deep in fallen leaves.

Fireplace, check. It's modern; I'm country. Sigh and check.

As I gazed at all the marks on the page, I realized the Lord had given me everything I had asked for. It was just packaged differently from what I had expected. Rather than seeing this house as a problem, I began to see it as a provision. And do you know what happened? I fell in love with this darling home.

I wonder how many times I've received from the Lord what I had asked for but just didn't recognize it?

P.S. Our home is on low ground, in town, and was a blue light opportunity!

23

Bucket Brigade

When I was growing up, my big brother Don had a favorite record he would play repeatedly. It was sung by Johnnie Ray and was entitled "The Little White Cloud That Cried." Over and over, that poor cloud would weep its little heart out. Just about the time you thought you couldn't bear to hear the cloud squeeze out one more teardrop, Don would turn the record over, and Johnnie would sing his hit song "Cry." We needed a bucket brigade just to handle the tears of this one crooner.

Some of you reading this will remember Johnnie Ray performing "Cry" on television. He would truly get into his song. Dramatically he would pull at his tie, open his shirt collar, drop to his knees, and finally fall to his face while pounding the floor with his fists. Don't you just love a man who can show emotion!

Okay, okay, maybe that's a little more emotion than I'd be comfortable with, but I wonder how many of us wouldn't benefit from a good gully wash.

While some of us have cried a river already, others of us have lost touch with this vital resource. I remember doing a retreat in central Georgia during which a number of tender and endearing things transpired that moved almost all of us gals to tears. But I spotted one young, attractive woman whose posture was like a robot's. She appeared to resist emotions positive or negative. I chatted with her and mentioned her "composure." She announced stoically, "I don't ever cry."

It was obvious she needed to, however, although I'm sure it would have been like releasing Niagara Falls. The torrent of tears would have eventually subsided, emptying out space for her to feel again.

I realize this crying thing can also be taken too far the other way. There's nothing sadder than a sniffing saint who's stuck inside herself and sees her sniveling as spiritual. Some soggy saints could be rented out as professional mourners. Grief was not meant to be an address but a process.

I used to think that because I cried so easily, I was deeply sensitive. Instead, I've learned that when someone told me a sad story, I was so full of my own unshed tears that the first tear I shed was for them, but the rest were for myself. Other people's pain kept tapping into my own unresolved issues.

I remember one night watching a movie on TV. Toward the end, the star was treated terribly by someone she loved. I felt her pain, and I began to cry. The story continued, and so did my tears. Building sobs were difficult to hold in. The movie ended, but I kept crying. My husband came into the room, and I blubbered, "I just feel so bad about that girl."

Tenderly Les said, "Honey, I don't think this is about that girl."

That did it. My dam burst! Les's words seemed to make it safe for me to feel my own pain. I began to realize that my first response was more than "sad movies make me cry." This girl's injury triggered my own buried memories. I wept and wailed for almost an hour. It was great! It wasn't great while I was crying—in fact, that was kind of scary. But the release I felt afterward was liberating.

Of course, most painful issues can't be resolved in an hour of crying, but many times it can be a good place to start.

Try this: List the last three times you cried. What did you cry about? Whom were you crying for?

Maybe you're a soggy saint. If so, it's time to call in a bucket brigade and get on with life.

Or maybe it's time for your tears, and you need someone to give you permission to let loose. Well, here it is. Go ahead . . . have a good, soul-washing cry!

24

Soup's On!

I hate feeling rejected. I'm so overwired in this area that when I approach a traffic signal and it turns red, I take it personally.

Okay, I'm not quite that sensitive, but I do like to be liked. I'm always grateful for the cheerleaders in my life—the people who root for me and believe the best about me. But into each person's life must come a few pom-pom pilferers.

I love speaking and have had the privilege of sharing the stage with many outstanding people. Usually we speakers are so busy that we don't have time to get to know each other. We fly into a city for an engagement, eat, speak, eat, talk with some of the audience personally, eat, and then go. (We leave with more "tonnage" than we came with!) I'm always overjoyed when I have a chance to "talk shop" with someone who shares the same type of ministry. So when a platform personality came to me after I spoke at a large event and wanted to chat, I was pleased.

She was warm and affirming and asked if she could recommend me to groups as she traveled. I was complimented and grateful. We chatted nonstop, then hugged and agreed to meet the following day for another visit before our departure.

When I met with her the next day, there seemed to be a problem. By her actions, I could tell I was it.

She went from cool to cold to curt. I went from confused to hurt to ticked. The ticked part came afterward, as I tried to figure out how I had fallen from favor. Later, I learned an acquaintance had spent some time with this speaker discussing me. I guess "Poached Patsy" didn't taste too good, because she certainly seemed to have indigestion.

The more I thought about the injustice of this encounter, the angrier I became. The incident stirred up memories of every unfair situation I'd ever experienced. I brooded, I boiled, and occasionally I blew up as I retold the story to Les. He got tired of receiving the residue of my rejection. So I set the incident on the back burner of my emotions and let it simmer. Once in a while, I'd lift the lid and stir the soup.

One day, while having lunch with cheerleading friends, the topic of unfair situations came up. I ran for the stove to check my pot, and sure enough, it was still hot. As I spewed my injustice all over them, they were taken aback by my intensity.

Finally one friend asked, "When did this happen?"

I had to stop and think for a moment, and then I realized it had been three years! My friends were surprised I still carried such animosity, because I had not seen this woman since that encounter.

After lunch, I thought through what my friends had said. I began to see that keeping this issue hot within me had left me with a pressure-cooker personality (minus the gauge). Instead of letting my rage diminish, I seemed to have used time to refine and define it.

Something about injustice convinces us of our right to hold
onto our anger and even embrace it. I'm learning anger is not
necessarily a wrong response . . . until I choose to harbor and
nurture it. When I enfold anger, it drains my energy and takes up
valuable inner space. Brewing anger taxes my physical, mental,
and emotional well-being. It also hampers my close relationships
with others and God.

Some of us don't have a handle on living skills that equips us
to deal with our emotions appropriately. We tend to deny we're
angry or defend our right to be so, leaving us frustrated, misun-
derstood, and stuck in the muck of our own emotions.

I understand now that the woman's momentary rejection of me
was not as damaging as my long-term choice to raise rage. When I
think of the people I have formed opinions of or changed my
opinions about because of what someone else has said, I'm aware
of what a human response it is—often not fair or loving, but
human.

When Les and I were first married, we lived in a mobile home
park. Just after we moved in, I was warned about the unfriendly
neighbor next door. I was told she kept to herself and was snob-
bish. Remembering what I had been told, it took me a while
before I tried to establish communication with her. It turned out
she was shy and very dear. She and I enjoyed a warm friendship
that I almost missed out on because someone had told me her
stunted understanding of my neighbor.

When the platform speaker and I had our puzzling encounter
that second day years ago, I felt hurt by her change of heart,
which is an appropriate feeling when you're rejected. But I
quickly put the lid over my hurt and turned up the burner of my
anger. Rejection felt too cold; at least anger had some self-gener-

ating warmth. But I must have stood too close to my own heat, because my emotions felt scorched. I'm slowly learning to take my hurts to the Healer before I hide them under my unrighteous rightness.

Relationships, like alphabet soup, spell out "opportunities." It's just that some are easier to swallow than others.

25

Fired Up!

Plucky: "Having or showing courage or spirited re-sourcefulness in trying circumstances" *(American Heritage Dictionary).*

Elijah was plucky. After all, he's the guy who challenged Ahab and Jezebel's wise guys to show up or shut up. Elijah laid out a game plan with the end result of winner takes all.

Allow me to set a little of the scene. (For inerrant accuracy, read 1 Kings 18 and 19.) Wicked Ahab, king of Israel, was miffed at Elijah for declaring a drought on the land and then disappearing. Ahab had searched the kingdom for three parched years, trying to find this troublemaker. Finally, Elijah sent a messenger to Ahab so they could have it out.

When they met, Ahab and Elijah began their finger-pointing meeting by blaming each other for Israel's problems. This was not your average my-daddy's-bigger-than-your-daddy argument. No, this was much bigger.

At that point in the debate, Elijah issued the divine dare. He invited Ahab's wise guys to a community barbecue and challenged them to a cook off. But listen to the plan: 850 wise guys against one fire-preaching prophet. If Elijah pulled it off, imagine the payoff on those kinds of odds!

Speaking of odd, the people thought this barbecue was a great idea. (I personally would not have wanted to go against a guy who spoke a drought into existence, but then I'm funny that way.)

The rules stated that the wise guys were to prepare an ox, lay it on the altar, and ask their gods to consume it in fire. Elijah would do the same and ask his God to send fire from heaven. The first one to smell fried ox (yuck!) wafting from his grill won.

The Baal and Asherah prophets pranced around the altar (similar to ring-around-the-rosy), trying to ignite a spark of enthusiasm from their gods. When they began to grow weary, Plucky Prophet Elijah taunted them: "I think your gods are out to lunch, nah, nah, nah, nah" (loose translation—very loose).

This brought a fresh surge of rage (you just can't kid with some people) and a renewed effort to kindle their gods' attention. But try as they might, the answer still appeared to be a big fat "Ho-hum."

Elijah was fired up. He positioned stones, prayed, and then watched the power of God consume the ox and everything surrounding it, including the dust. (Do you know how difficult it is to burn dirt?) The fire-licking flames even lapped up water and sizzled the surroundings bone dry.

Remember the odds? They changed. The barbecue turned into an evangelistic meeting, and no one had even sung 13 choruses of a favorite hymn. The people fell on their faces and acknowledged the one true God. Elijah took it from there and wiped out the wise guys.

Elijah's barbecue was a blazing success. That is, until . . .

Word arrived, via Ahab, to Queenie. To say Jezebel was not happy to hear she'd missed the big event of the year would be to understate this sinister woman's fury. She faxed her seething sentiments to Elijah, outlining her outrage, and he hot-footed it into the hills.

Excuse me? What happened to our plucky powerhouse who took on a passel of prophets? Surely one wicked woman couldn't douse our fiery prophet's ministry. Could she? Was this another case of "never underestimate the power of a woman"? I think not. Looked more like a slump in emotions following a big event.

Our fading hero ended up knee knocking under a juniper, singing a familiar refrain in the key of "me." He whined so long that he wore himself out and fell fast asleep.

I love the next part of the story. Here was a wayward man, battling self-pity and anguish, headed in the wrong direction, and the Lord sent him company and provision. An angel woke him and offered him a cake. (Wow! Angel food cake, one of my favorites.)

Elijah, a man after my own weakness, ate and fell back asleep. But the Lord of the second chance awakened our friend again, fed him, and allowed him to continue his journey. The heavenly host's cooking was so vitamin-enriched that Elijah went on in the strength of it for 40 days. (I'd sure like that recipe, although I've cooked some meals my family hoped I wouldn't fix again for 40 days. Does that count?)

Even with two chances, Elijah's fears didn't diminish. Instead of turning back, he scampered away. He eventually hid in the side of a mountain. He caved in emotionally. (I wonder if he was agoraphobic.) He trusted in a rocky fortress instead of the Fortress who is our Rock.

Once again, our God pursued the lost, the lonely, the confused, the fearful, the deceived. In a gentle breeze, He whispered His loving direction to our fleeing friend. Elijah heard, returned, and for his grand finale joined the Lord in a blaze of victory.

I don't identify with many of Elijah's strengths, although I once set my dish towel on fire while cooking lamb chops. What I connect with are his weaknesses. I'm reminded how susceptible we are emotionally to the threats of the enemy, especially following spiritual conquest.

I have made some of my worst personal bungles following some of my sweetest spiritual advancements. For me, I think pride edged in, and I tripped over it. But I'm convinced we need more than luck in this life. We also need pluck. And I know of only one reliable Source for that kind of character.

26

LOW · NORMAL · HOT

Bouquet

I am a woman who loves getting presents. Fortunately, I'm married to a man who gets a kick out of buying me surprises. He also is famous, in a spontaneous moment, for whisking me off to a mall to shop for a new outfit. It's not unusual for us to go into a dress shop and have Les want to buy more for me than I would for myself. That causes quite a reaction from the sales clerks, since his attitude is not the norm. They all want to know how I trained Les to be that way. Unfortunately, I can't take credit. (I love credit, too.) He just has that kind of giving heart.

I remember our nineteenth wedding anniversary, when Les wrote me a funny, little poem that I still cherish.

Roses are red, violets are blue,

If I had it to do over again,

I'd still marry you!

The poem was especially dear to me because Les and I married when we were 17 and 18, and we had been through some challenging years (financially, physically, and emotionally), including my period of agoraphobia. From time to time, I wondered if he regretted his choice. So even though the poem didn't exactly start off originally, it ended for me like a masterpiece.

Over the years (30), Les has given me gifts that have made me laugh, cry, gasp, and even learn some lessons.

One sunny, spring day, Les came bounding into our home embracing two apricot sweetheart rosebuds for me. I, of course, was delighted.

The flowers had come with a powdered mix to lengthen their blooming time; I stirred it into the water. I gave each rose a fresh cut and then slipped them into one of the many vases collected from Les's continued courting of me. I sat my mini-bouquet in the living room, being careful to protect it from direct sun and yet giving it visibility for my enjoyment.

As the days went by, I was fascinated by what happened. My seemingly identical roses responded very differently to their environment. One began slowly to open, and at each stage of development, she was exquisite. Her unfolding presentation pleased me and added beauty and wonder to the room. Finally, my apricot beauty dropped her petals in a breathtaking farewell performance.

In contrast, the other rose seemed stuck in her beginning. She held tenaciously to her baby form. In the end, the brooding bud turned brown and hung over the edge of the vase like a tragic teardrop.

For days I thought about the contrasting visual. I've always applauded rosebuds as being so romantic. Yet there was something sad and unnatural about seeing a flower begin and end at the same place. The bud that didn't open never reached her potential. She never released the sweet fragrance placed within her to share with others. Her death portrayed regret and sadness.

I could celebrate even the loss of the open rose, knowing she accomplished all she was designed to do. Her fragrance lingered in our home even after the vase was removed.

My friend Vella was a flower in the fullest sense. When she was told she had only a short time to live and that her cancer was the most painful of cancers, instead of closing up, she spread her petals all the way open and bathed us in the fragrance of faith. We would not have blamed her if she had drawn into a bud and died privately in her pain.

But Vella saw this illness as her farewell performance, an opportunity for as long as she had left to fulfill the design God had for her. Vella lived out her remaining days with exquisite grace. Dropping her last petal, her parting words were, "Praise the Lord." Then she fell asleep and was gone.

Family and friends could celebrate her life and her homegoing. At the time of this writing, it has been 11 years since she left us . . . and her fragrance still lingers.

Because there's a great deal of cancer in my family, I sometimes wonder how I would handle it if I were to be diagnosed with the dreaded disease. I'm not a brave person . . . except in my imagination. There I am valiant, noble, and steadfast. In reality, I whine when I get a cold.

Three years ago, I watched my dear, 73-year-old mother endure breast surgery for cancer. She went through her diagnoses, surgery, and radiation not only with courage, but also with sweetness and humor. That gave me hope.

I want, whatever my environment, to be growing and fragrant. I don't want to be closed and unable emotionally to open up to others. I don't want to die holding to myself what I should have given away.

Les's gift of roses, pressed between the pages of my memory, has been a poignant reminder: Openness is a risk, growth is its reward, and His grace makes it all possible.

27

Seasonal Seesaw

I love the holidays!

I hate the holidays!

I am a Christmas contradiction. I'm up with excitement and then down with disappointment. I'm up with anticipation and then down with depression. I'm up with . . . well, you get the idea. I'm on my seasonal seesaw. My teeter-totter partner is my own Currier-and-Ives expectations.

Ever notice in those Currier and Ives pictures how even in frigid weather the cows are contented? They willingly pose next to the wood for the fireplace, which is neatly stacked next to the house. While Bossy grins, Junior is shown joyfully skipping out to bring Mother dear kindling for the stove.

I don't have a cow, but I do have a dog. Pumpkin refuses to go outside if it's damp. She has an aversion to moist feet. She will sit for days with her paws crossed, waiting for the sun or wind to dry up the ground. No way is she going to pose willingly by a wet wood pile.

Of course, that would be difficult anyway since we don't have any wood—that is, unless I hike five miles to the woods and gnaw off a few branches. Oh, well, our fireplace stays cleaner that way.

I tried to imagine our Junior skipping joyfully toward a task outside in inclement weather. Ha! I think Junior caught Pumpkin's malady.

No matter how I try, I can't seem to cram my family onto the front of one of those cards.

I don't know why I can't remember, from one Christmas season to the next, that Currier and Ives is an unattainable height. Every Christmas, I want my house to be picture perfect. Ha! I can't achieve that in a nonholiday time, much less in a season with so many added demands.

I imagine white birch logs (cut by me in our back 40—feet, that is) snuggled in a handwoven basket (I designed) placed next to the hearth. The blazing fire invites guests to warm in our candle-lit (all hand-dipped by me) dining room. I would serve a gourmet dinner for 30, followed by strolling musicians playing Handel's "Messiah." All this would take place in my 10-by-12 dining area.

When I have such unreasonable goals, I end up with a high frustration level and a frazzled nervous system. Then I find myself in last-minute panic spurts, trying to excuse, hide, and disguise all my unfinished projects.

One year we decided to write Noel in lights on our house. We started late and finished only half the project because of bad weather. That left a multi-colored NO flashing on our rooftop. We had fewer guests that year.

Usually, I wait too long to complete my shopping, leaving me victim to jangled nerves from holiday traffic, crowds, and checkout lines. People's personalities are seldom enhanced under pressure. Also, I tend to be more impulsive in my buying when I'm running late. I suffer from bargain whiplash trying to take advantage of all the Christmas markdowns. Too many last-minute purchases leave me holding the bag . . . and it's full of bills. The bills then pile up in my emotions, leaving me feeling spent.

Also, during the holiday hoopla I seem to get bit by the bug. No, not the flu bug; the love bug. I fall into the trap of thinking everyone is going to get along. Give me a break! How unrealistic to believe relatives and friends, some of whom have never hit it off, would suddenly become seasonal sidekicks! I'm learning there are those who believe "Ho, Ho, Ho" is something you do strictly in your garden and has nothing to do with exhibiting a merry heart.

Another habit I have is wanting everyone to love the gifts I give them as much as I did when I selected them. I'm into applause and appreciation. Here's the problem: I live with three guys (one husband and two sons), and they only applaud silly things like grand slam home runs in the World Series, touchdowns in the final seconds of the Super Bowl, or when I fix dinner and they can tell what it is.

They don't show the same enthusiasm for my gifts—like the nifty button extenders, the monogrammed electric socks, or the fuchsia-colored long johns I wrapped for them. I realize my gifts are . . . uh . . . distinctive, but I want them to be memorable. My guys agree they have been.

Well, there it is, my Christmas confession. Maybe some of you can identify with part, if not all, of my seasonal seesaw. Come join me in entering into the holidays without the teeter and totter in our emotions. Here's how:

1. Set more-sane house goals. Better to plan less and accomplish more than to fall short of your ideal and start your holidays

feeling disappointed.

2. Shop early, and buy a couple of generic emergency gifts. (Unlike fuchsia underwear, a box of fine chocolates holds general appeal.)

3. Settle on a reasonable budget before going into the stores to prevent falling victim to strong sales tactics (which include Christmas mood music that plays on our nostalgia, sale-sign seduction, and plastic explosives in the form of credit cards).

4. Sow the seeds of goodwill, but don't expect every "Scrooge" in your Christmas circle to embrace your efforts . . . or you, for that matter. Don't snowball your own emotions by expecting love from people who can't give it. (History in a relationship is usually a good benchmark of his or her ability.)

5. Seek some silence. Balance your busyness with moments of meditation. Don't allow all the flashing lights on the outside to distract you from the inner light of His presence. Even a short silence each day will give a greater semblance of order to your emotions and schedule.

Set goals, shop early, settle budget, sow goodwill,

seek silence,

and don't forget to

SIMPLY CELEBRATE!

Ways to celebrate simply:

Make a snow angel, drink eggnog, write a forgotten friend, decorate a snowman, go caroling in your neighborhood, feed the birds, bake apples, watch the movies *Heidi* and *Little Women,* write a poem, cut out cookies, share tea with a friend, frame an old snapshot, hug a child, hug an oldster, read the Christmas story out loud, and sing Happy Birthday to Jesus.

28

Eek!

Y'all come, hear," is music to my ears. I love knee-slappin', banjo-pickin', harmonica-playin', good ol' country livin'.

Every summer when I was a youngster, my family would travel south to the Bluegrass State to "sit a spell." We had more relatives in Madisonville and Nebo, Kentucky, than a corncob has kernels.

One of my favorite places to go was my Aunt Pearl's. She was feisty and funny, and she made visiting her memorable.

I remember one visit when I stayed alone with Aunt Pearl. Usually one of her four children was around, but not this time. Even though I was a teenager, when it came time for bed, I didn't want to sleep by myself. She lived out of town, and I was a city slicker not used to the wide-open, dark countryside.

Aunt Pearl was a down-home girl who knew how to make people feel welcome and comfortable. She had me crawl right in bed with her.

We had said good night, and I was listening to the outside night sounds, about to doze off, when an inside noise caught my attention.

It sounded as if someone or something was scratching frantically.

"Aunt Pearl," I whispered.

"Huh?" she groaned from her half-conscious rest.

"What's that noise?" I whimpered.

"I dunno," she slurred.

I realized I was losing her to sleep, and I needed to know what that frightening sound was. So I gently shook her arm and called, "Aunt Pearl, Aunt Pearl, listen."

Coming to, she lifted her head, eyes still closed, and listened. Then, from years of experience, she stated, "It's okay. It's only a mouse that has fallen off the kitchen counter into the garbage can."

Only! Only! She might as well have said, "It's okay, it's only Big Foot." I don't do mice. I was petrified.

Much to my amazement and horror, my aunt laid her head back on her pillow instead of getting up and calling 911.

"Aunt Pearl, aren't you going to do something?" I questioned.

"What do you want me to do?"

"I'm not sure. Call someone maybe."

She laughed, rose up, and headed for the kitchen. I heard some shuffling around, and the scratching stopped. Within minutes, she was climbing back into bed.

"What did you do?" I puzzled.

"Oh, I opened the door and dumped him out into the night. Now go to sleep."

"Okay," I responded, trying to imagine anyone so brave as to have deliberately gone close to a monster in a mouse suit.

Within moments, my aunt began to snore. But in between the

short and long snoring sounds, I heard something. It sounded like frantic scratching.

"Aunt Pearl, Aunt Pearl, please wake up," I pleaded.

"Now what?" she said groggily.

"Did you close the door before you came to bed? I think that mouse is back."

"Just go to sleep. That mouse ain't botherin' you."

I listened to its attempt to escape its paper prison. Then I told her, "You're wrong. That mouse is bothering me a lot."

She swung her legs out of bed, grabbed her slipper, and left the room. Another minute passed. Then I heard a couple of thuds followed by silence. My aunt hurried back to our room, dropped her slipper next to the bed, and climbed in.

Wide-eyed I said, "What did you do?"

"I killed it," she replied calmly.

"Killed it!" I cringed. "With what?"

"My slipper," she reported as she rolled away from me.

Now I was nauseated. I had wanted the mouse excommunicated, not executed. I could hardly stand the thought that I was sleeping in the same room with the weapon that was probably covered in mouse particles. I wanted to go home.

As I was trying to figure out how to tell my aunt I needed to leave immediately, I heard a now-familiar sound. I wondered if this mouse had swallowed a cat and therefore had nine lives. It scrambled around in the garbage bag and evidently was trying to leap out, as we heard it falling repeatedly.

This time I didn't have to say anything. My aunt marched through the house, determined to put my fears to bed, as well as herself. I heard the back door slam, and then her footsteps as she made a beeline for her bed.

When her head dropped onto the pillow, she announced, "The can, the bag, the slipper, and the mouse are outside, and the door is closed and locked. Good night."

I scooched closer to her and fell sound asleep.

Today I still have fears dressed in Big Foot suits. Often these fears grow larger in the night as I lie awake and hear them vigorously stomping around my house. I sometimes find myself whimpering, but now I cry to the Lord. Again and again, I've found Him faithful to respond, and the closer I move to Him, the safer I feel and the better I rest.

29

TNT

fter dinner one night, my friend turned, looked intently at me, and stated gently, "Do you know what I see when I look in your eyes?"

"Blue?" I quipped.

"Anger," she responded.

"Anger!" I exploded with venom. "Anger! You don't see any anger in me! You might see fear, but not anger."

I went home that night ticked! As I stomped through the house, I bellowed out to the heavens, "Who does she think she is?"

At that point, I noticed my clenched fist flailing around in midair. I stood for a moment, staring at this volatile visual. As I opened my fist, I saw imprints deeply etched in my palms by my fingernails. I asked aloud, "Am I angry, Lord?"

Immediately my mind was catapulted back to years before when I had a panic attack after a spat with Les. The attack was terrifying. I decided it wasn't safe to get angry (an old message that was now reinforced). I had pushed down deeper inside of me some unresolved anger issues, and what came up to take their place was unrelenting guilt and unreasonable fear—I had become one of the "un" generation. That gruesome twosome, guilt and fear, dominated my life for a number of years.

When I began to deal with my guilt and fear through the wise counsel of Scripture and friends, I thought emotionally I was going to be home free. I believed I would finally be normal. Instead, without the cover of the gruesome twosome, my now-volcanic anger had begun to erupt toward those around me.

I discovered different kinds of anger. There's the temporarily-ticked kind in which we want to yank a hank of hair off someone's head, but only for a moment. There's the slow sizzle style in which we work overtime on the details of the offense and then revel in our wrath. A favorite of many is the dump-truck approach. This is when we back up to a person and unload all our "stuff" on them. Following close is the rage routine, sung to the tune of "I'm going to hate you forever . . . or at least until Jesus returns."

My sister, Elizabeth, saw the dump-truck approach at work in her own home. She had just finished a phone call and found that her three-year-old son, Nicholas, had been making use of his "free" time. He had sprinkled two pounds of flour laced with Kool-Aid powder throughout the living room. After a firm scolding from his mom, Nicholas, indignant that his culinary endeavors had not been appreciated, trucked into the playroom and hit his two-year-old sister, Lindsey.

I can identify. There have been times when I've released a flurry of fury at some unsuspecting soul, surprising, at times, both of us. I've learned that when I haven't dealt with my emotions and they stockpile, I will inappropriately dump them on an unsuspecting bystander—like a checkout clerk, a bank teller, or a waitress.

I remember trucking over to a receptionist for a mistake on a billing. She was calm and kind. I, on the other hand, was spitting words through tight teeth and displaying pulsating purple veins. The good news was that I had more color than I usually do. The bad news was that my faith faded fast in the eyes of this young woman. Even though I returned and apologized, it changed our relationship. She is far more reserved than she once was with me . . . and rightfully so.

The results of dump-trucking on an innocent party are that it leaves them on-guard, and they skirt around any meaningful involvement with us. It takes a lot of time and effort to reestablish a relationship. Even if we don't care to reinstate a connection, that type of dump-'em-and-leave-'em behavior runs over our chances of having any personal integrity.

I wasn't that put out with the receptionist's mistake when I "let her have it." My reaction came following a disagreement with a relative in which I had shoveled my feelings into the back of my dumpster instead of saying how I felt. Then, when the botched-up bill came, I jumped into my rig, backed my truck up to the receptionist's desk, and unloaded my cargo right in her lap.

I'm learning that as long as I misdirect my emotions, I will find myself rationalizing my TNT behavior and limiting my ability to have honest relationships.

30

LOW · NORMAL · HOT

Overnight Fright

I was booked on an early-morning flight out of Detroit on my way to Iowa. Because I was leaving before daybreak, Les and I decided to stay at a hotel near the airport the night before. We had done this on several occasions and found it less stressful. I didn't have to get up early and therefore would be more rested, and Les didn't have to battle the morning rush-hour traffic.

We arrived at the hotel and checked in. Somehow our request to be on the first floor had been mixed up, and instead we had a third-floor room. Les and I decided we could adjust. We wouldn't allow a room change to ruin our evening.

We had an early dinner that was not good enough to recommend and yet not poor enough to send back. After our mediocre meal, we retired to our room to relax.

I kicked off my shoes and began to leaf through a newspaper. Les remembered seeing a pop machine and thought he would buy a few sodas for us. He was gone quite a while, and when he returned he was shaking his head. He had visited three different soda machines, and the change makers were broken on all of them. He then checked at the front desk, and they were unable to provide him with change. So we settled for ice water.

Then we noticed the red message light was flashing on the phone. I buzzed the desk and asked for the message. It was for a Mr. Hudson from a business associate. I assured the gal I was not Mr. Hudson and asked if she would please turn off the red blinker. She said she would.

I organized what I would be wearing on the flight the following day and decided to go to bed. I whipped back the bedspread and top sheet so I could crawl in. Much to my disgust, the sheets were dirty. They looked grungy, and every square inch was wrinkled. I wondered if these were Mr. Hudson's sheets. If so, he had left wisps of his brunette tresses and makeup behind.

I called the desk and reported the need for clean linens. The girl at the desk apologized and said someone would come with fresh bedding. Well, someone came all right . . . the Sheet Inspector.

The (six-foot-five) Sheet Inspector announced he had come to inspect our sheets. (Of course, we should have known.) He approached the bed, looked closely at the sheets, then made his way slowly around to the other side of the bed, still examining. (To have an in-house inspector made me think ours may not have been their first sheet complaint.)

After contemplating for a moment, he announced, "These sheets are dirty."

I wondered how much he got paid for linen appraisal. I'd been thinking about a part-time position. It was obvious I qualified, since we both had come to the same conclusion.

As the inspector left, he took our sheets and promised to return soon. He kept his word. He returned promptly. We opened the door and found out that Sheet Inspectors must be specialists, because he handed us our linens and marched away.

Les and I stood looking at each other in disbelief, then shrugged our shoulders and resigned ourselves to the bed-making task. To expedite this project, we each got on one side of the bed, and Les flung one corner of the sheet over to me. I caught it, and then I gasped. Les looked, and his eyes dropped in disgust. These were the same sheets we had before.

We called the desk, and the girl told us she would lodge a written complaint to housekeeping. Now, not only did I have grungy sheets, but I also had developed an attitude the size of the inspector.

When it registered that they were not planning to bring us clean sheets in the near future, I became creative. I gathered all the clean towels and spread them lengthwise on the bed, giving us a somewhat nappy but clean sleeping surface. Then we climbed in bed, and I fell asleep despite the message light flashing in my face, still beckoning Mr. Hudson.

I woke up off and on throughout the night. I couldn't seem to get the looped threads in the towels to go all in the same direction. I dreamt that the Sheet Inspector came back to our room dressed in red blinking pillowcases and fined us for sleeping on the towels.

Finally morning arrived (Mr. Hudson's light was still flickering), and we could hardly wait to leave. We certainly were not rested. *Tested* would be more like it. I can't tell you how difficult it was to leave, knowing we had paid for this stress-filled night.

I'm sure you're wondering why we didn't demand retribution. We did . . . eventually. When the time was right.

You see, the day before the hotel havoc, Les had gone through a heart catheterization. He had just found out he had had a second heart attack and that one of his bypasses had closed. We checked into the hotel (part of a reputable chain) to protect him from stress while he was recovering. When we ended up in "The Hotel from Hell," we had to weigh which was more important: fighting for what we paid for, or adapting and filing a complaint at a more appropriate time.

Believe me, demanding my rights would have been far easier for my temperament. But when I weighed the battle with the hotel against my husband's well-being, what was one uncomfortable night?

Too many times in my life, I have reacted from my emotions rather than from wisdom. Wisdom says, "There is . . . a time to be silent and a time to speak" (Eccles. 3:1, 7*b*).

I don't think it's a mistake that silence is listed before speaking. Usually if we wait, we're more likely to handle ourselves and our words with greater dignity.

After returning from my speaking trip, I did call the hotel's headquarters. They were surprised to find they had a Sheet Inspector working for them. They refunded our money and sent us a coupon for a free night at the same hotel. Harrumph! Not in this lifetime.

I sure hope Mr. Hudson received his message.

31

Bedded Bliss

When we moved into our new home, I could hardly wait to decorate. I started with our bedroom. It was a generous-size room and showed potential. All I had to do was coordinate the decor.

Our aging bedspread had served us well but needed to be relieved of duty. Selecting colors and a pattern for our new spread was great fun. I chose a multicolored comforter. The saleswoman pointed out the matching shams and sheets. Les and I hadn't thought about an ensemble . . . but it would be nice.

As we were getting ready to pay for our mound of goods, the sales gal pulled out a wallpaper book to show us the paper designed just for our bedding. It was beautiful. I *had* planned to wallpaper . . . eventually. Besides, if I didn't get this now, I might never find another paper that would fit so perfectly.

As Les and I left the store with our arms full of parcels, we were elated, in a heavy sort of way. We comforted and buoyed each other with the thoughts "It's not like we've ever done this before" and "We just won't spend as much for the living room."

When we arrived home, I immediately put the bedding on, and we oohed and ahhed it. Then, after the wallpaper was hung, we were even more pleased with the coordinated look we had achieved. But I had failed to think through the pictures on the walls. They didn't fit in well. I could always bring some in from another room or buy some cheapies.

As I was hanging my newly purchased pictures beside my bed, I noticed how tacky the table cover was on my nightstand. It just didn't fit with everything else. How much could a little cover cost, anyway? Actually, more than I had anticipated.

We had invested a lot, but at least my room was in harmony with itself . . . except for the bath that opened into the bedroom. It seemed visually disruptive. After hanging an antique mirror and lace shower curtains and adding a looped rug, my pocketbook was empty, but my eyes were full of continuity.

As I studied my endeavors, it hit me that I could enhance my efforts with multiple pillows and some flowers. Those two additions are the way a woman places her finishing touches on a room. I added eight pillows and a bouquet of silk roses. Yes, yes, these were like a feminine signature . . . and with a few candles would be complete.

I must have overdone the candles, because Les installed a smoke detector. But the candles seemed necessary to add ambience. Our bedroom would have been a masterpiece, but it seemed to need an injection of character. I dragged in Les's grandfather's trunk and set it at the foot of our bed. That worked. I displayed an antique wicker tray on the top of the trunk. The tray required just a few small, framed photographs, a teapot, a pair of women's gloves, and a man's pocket watch to create a still-life effect.

Funny I could be that far into our bedroom project and only

then notice how out of place my lamps looked. Totally the wrong feeling, and even the shape seemed passé. It would be a shame to allow them to rob us of the rewards of all our time and toil. Lamps are small in stature but big in impact. Once you flick on one of those babies, you can't help but notice it.

Speaking of noticing . . . I have worked so intently with this room that I've developed a new problem. I'm tired of the whole thing and wish I could start over.

When is enough . . . enough?

32

Awakening

Hello, Patsy. This is your sister, and I thought you should know that I am very sick."

When I hung up from Elizabeth's call, I immediately prayed on her behalf. Thoughts of her would come to me again and again over the next 24 hours, and I would quietly pray and then go on with my day. Even though I could tell from Elizabeth's weak, quivering voice that she was ill, I was not prepared for the next call.

This time it was my brother-in-law, Bryan. He reported in disbelief that in the night, Elizabeth's fever had gone up and she was shaking uncontrollably, so he had taken her to the hospital. By the time they arrived at the emergency room, she had become disoriented. The nurses helped her into bed, and Elizabeth went into a coma.

The doctors weren't sure what was wrong with her, but her brain was swelling. I was devastated. How could this be?

Seventeen years prior, our 39-year-old brother had died of a brain injury following a car accident. The thought of losing my

33-year-old sister through some sort of brain problem seemed more than I could bear. It just didn't seem normal that our family would have to go through a second tragic loss of this type.

Another call came informing us that Elizabeth had been placed on life support and was now listed in critical condition.

Her voice kept replaying in my ear: "Patsy, I just thought you should know that I am very sick."

Waves of realization would flood in on me, and I would reel from the impact. Then I would busy myself, only to have another wave crash down on me.

Tears came like raindrops that soon built to what felt like tidal waves racking my body. I was overwhelmed.

Bryan called again to report there was no response from Elizabeth, even to pain. "Patsy, I just feel that if you would come, she would be able to hear your voice," he choked out through his tears.

When I hung up, I told Les that Bryan's belief she could hear me was that of a desperate man longing to have his wife and the mother of their three young children back. I knew the days of Elizabeth's life were in God's hands and that I could not add to or subtract from them.

"Yes," Les agreed, "but God often uses people to speak."

I knew that was true because of all the times the Lord has given me insight, counsel, and encouragement through the voices of people. Some of my reluctance to go to her bedside was self-protective. I didn't feel I could handle flying out to Utah to see her die. But Les's tender reminder caused me to make plans to leave as soon as we could.

The closer our plane got to the Salt Lake City airport, the calmer and stronger I felt. Upon arriving, we rented a car and drove immediately to the hospital, half an hour away.

When we got there, we tried to prepare ourselves for what Elizabeth might look like. Much to our surprise, she looked quite well, even with all the life-support equipment. But our hearts and hopes dropped when we touched her. Her skin felt like wax, and her limbs were ice-water cold.

I was heartsick when the intensive care nurse came in with a rounded pair of scissors and pressed them as hard as she could into Elizabeth's cuticles on her fingers and toes. Elizabeth gave no response.

Sleep was skimpy for Les and me that night. We grabbed some breakfast and headed for the hospital at the first light of dawn. Then we took turns talking to Elizabeth and asking her to give us some sign that she could hear us.

At one point, Les was sure she put some pressure on his hand with hers, but it didn't happen again. Several times that day, her eyes seemed to be trying to open, but the nurses said it was an involuntary movement of a comatose patient. We watched the countless machines and computer printouts, trying to analyze what it all meant.

That evening, we went back to our room for another long, fitful night.

The following afternoon, I was alone, sitting next to Elizabeth's bed, and started to talk to her about when she was a little girl. (I was 13 when she was born, and I felt very motherly toward her. Translated, that means I was bossy and protective.) I was telling her about the time she gave her stuffed monkey, JoJo, a bath in the toilet and then threw her moist monkey and our mom's poodle in the dryer. Fortunately, both JoJo and Sassy survived.

All of a sudden, I realized Elizabeth's eyes were darting around under her closed eyelids. There wasn't a nurse around to ask about it, so I leaned in to my sister's ear and said, "Elizabeth, it would really help me to know if you can hear me. If you can hear me, would you please open your eyes?"

I cannot begin to tell you how I felt as I saw her eyes open fully to my request. In that moment, hope surged through me like electricity. Even though I could tell she couldn't see, I now knew she could hear, understand, process, and respond.

I flew out to the nurses' station and excitedly reported what had happened. The nurse looked at me as though I had said, "There is dust on the windowsill."

Realizing my own nervousness, I figured I hadn't spoken clearly. I deliberately slowed down my speech and retold my story. The nurse looked at me and simply stated, "That did not happen. I have been taking care of her for the past ten hours, and she is incapable of responding."

Then her voice softened. "Families tend to overreact to patients' involuntary movements."

"Trust me," I insisted. "She responded on command."

"As far as I'm concerned, that never happened," she stated flatly, then walked away.

I sulked back to my sister's room and stood silently at her bedside, mulling over what had happened and what was said.

About then, the nurse came in to check the equipment. I looked at her and then at Elizabeth.

I moved close to Elizabeth's ear and pleaded, "I know I've been bugging you a lot today, but I need you to leave that quiet place where you're resting, and I need you to open your eyes. I want you to open them wide, and I want you to do it right now!"

As I said "now," the nurse looked nonchalantly over her shoulder toward my sister. Elizabeth's eyes popped open like an owl's. My hope surged! And the nurse? She almost fainted. After catching her breath, she scurried to the phone to alert the doctor.

By the next morning, when I spoke Elizabeth's name, she not only heard me, but she also knew me and almost jumped into my arms.

It took days for all the equipment to be removed and for her vocal cords to heal enough from the trauma of her breathing tubes that she could talk. Then she told us that the first thing she could remember was my voice calling her name and talking to her as though she were a young child.

Weeks later, as I looked back, I began to see how my responses to my sister's illness were like the flowers I harvest from my garden. When a bloom is cut from the plant, the stem seals the severed area to preserve the moisture it contains. This self-protective action prevents the flower from taking in any additional water. So while the sealing is an attempt to preserve life, it also keeps the plant from receiving sustenance from sources such as water in a vase. For this reason, florists instruct buyers to make a fresh cut in the stem and immediately place it in water to extend its life.

When I first received word about Elizabeth, I, like the flower, felt as though I had to seal my resources within myself to survive. I had just come through an emotionally and physically draining season of my life that had left me feeling incapable of dealing with this crisis.

But when Les suggested God could somehow speak through me even though I felt so fragile, it was as if someone had made a fresh cut and placed me in water. Deciding I could go to Utah and survive—whatever the outcome—gave me a quiet strength. That strength grew every day.

I wasn't strong because of any special wisdom or stamina within myself, but because I had been plunged into the water of the Great Sustainer.

It was an important lesson on human nature and divine intervention. All in all, I feel fortunate to have been a part of Elizabeth's awakening and to have learned how He restores us by His living water when we would wilt without Him.

Life often comes at us with TNT force, leaving us emotionally tentative and spiritually bewildered. Our circumstances often don't seem fair and certainly don't appear to be normal.

My quest for normalcy has brought me to the understanding that our commonality is in our abnormality. The good news is that that's okay. We are unique, which beats normal any day. In fact, we are so amazingly designed that God supervised the placement of our inner workings and registered our existence even before we were held for the first time. Then He who formed us takes His involvement a step further and uses our circumstances in our best interests. That leaves us free to embrace the fact that normal . . . is just a setting on your dryer.

Take a Lighthearted Look at Life . . .
with these other books by Patsy Clairmont!

I Love Being a Woman

Join Patsy on a whirlwind tour of women in the Bible that we can learn from today: Esther, Ruth, Abigail and more. Weaving wisdom in alongside her witty observations, Patsy celebrates the unique qualities that make womanhood wonderful. Paperback and book-on-cassette.

God Uses Cracked Pots

How does God best reveal Himself in us? When we allow His light to shine through the broken places of our lives. With many hilarious and a few embarrassing tales of a self-proclaimed "cracked pot," Patsy Clairmont encourages readers to take themselves a little less seriously and enjoy life to the fullest, as He intended. Paperback and book-on-cassette.

Sportin' a 'Tude

Patsy's back, and she's better than ever! And readers will be smiling in agreement as she takes a good look at our attitudes and what they communicate to others. In her typical honest, light-hearted manner, Patsy reveals the many ways our attitudes speak volumes—*especially* when we're not looking—to point us toward the one 'tude we should display: the attitude of Christ. Paperback and book-on-cassette.

. . .

Look for these books in your favorite Christian bookstore. You can also request a copy by calling 1-800-A-FAMILY or by writing Focus on the Family, Colorado Springs, CO 80995. Friends in Canada may call 1-800-661-9800 or write Focus on the Family, P.O. Box 9800, Stn. Terminal, Vancouver, B.C. V6B 4G3. Visit our Web site—www.family.org—to learn more about the ministry or to find out if there is a Focus on the Family office in your country.

subject to availability

9PBXRTH

FOCUS ON THE FAMILY®

*W*elcome to the *F*amily!

Whether you received this book as a gift, borrowed it from
a friend, or purchased it yourself, we're glad you read it! It's just
one of the many helpful, insightful and encouraging
resources produced by Focus on the Family.

In fact, that's what Focus on the Family is all about—providing inspira-
tion, information and biblically based advice to people in all stages of life.

It began in 1977 with the vision of one man, Dr. James Dobson, a licensed
psychologist and author of 16 best-selling books on marriage, parenting,
and family. Alarmed by the societal, political, and economic pressures
that were threatening the existence of the American family, Dr. Dobson
founded Focus on the Family with one employee—an assistant—
and a once-a-week radio broadcast, aired on only 36 stations.

Now an international organization, Focus on the Family is dedicated
to preserving Judeo-Christian values and strengthening the family
through more than 70 different ministries, including eight separate
daily radio broadcasts; television public service announcements;
11 publications; and a steady series of books and award-winning
films and videos for people of all ages and interests.

Recognizing the needs of, as well as the sacrifices and important
contribution made by, such diverse groups as educators, physicians,
attorneys, crisis pregnancy center staff and single parents,
Focus on the Family offers specific outreaches to uphold and
minister to these individuals, too. And it's all done for one purpose,
and one purpose only: to encourage and strengthen individuals
and families through the life-changing message of Jesus Christ.

• • •

For more information about the ministry, or if we can be of help to your
family, simply write to Focus on the Family, Colorado Springs, CO 80995
or call 1-800-A-FAMILY (1-800-232-6459). Friends in Canada may write
Focus on the Family, P.O. Box 9800, Stn. Terminal, Vancouver, B.C. V6B 4G3
or call 1-800-661-9800. Visit our Web site—www.family.org—
to learn more about the ministry or to find out if there is a
Focus on the Family office in your country.

We'd love to hear from you!